Ajit Singh
Amrita Prakash

Metaverse
Simply In Depth

MetaVerse *Simply In Depth*

For information about this title or to order other books and/or electronic media, contact the publisher:

Ajit Singh & Amrita Prakash

PREFACE

Welcome to the world of the metaverse, a realm where imagination knows no bounds and possibilities are limitless. This book invites you on a captivating journey into the metaverse, a concept that has captivated the minds of visionaries, futurists, and technologists alike.

The metaverse represents a convergence of virtual reality, augmented reality, artificial intelligence, blockchain, and other cutting-edge technologies. It transcends the boundaries of physical reality, opening up a new dimension where virtual worlds come alive, and where individuals can connect, create, and collaborate in ways never before imagined.

In this book, we explore the origins, concepts, technologies, and applications that make up the metaverse. We delve into the historical development of the metaverse, tracing its roots in science fiction and its emergence as a tangible concept in our digital age. We uncover the core characteristics and foundational technologies that underpin the metaverse, shedding light on the building blocks that bring this immersive world to life.

Throughout the chapters, we examine the metaverse's impact on various sectors and domains, from entertainment and gaming to education, healthcare, finance, and beyond. We explore the transformative potential of the metaverse, envisioning a future where virtual and physical realities seamlessly merge, fostering creativity, collaboration, and new avenues of exploration.

But the metaverse is not without its challenges. We address the ethical considerations, privacy concerns, and societal implications that arise as we navigate this digital frontier. We discuss the importance of inclusivity, accessibility, and responsible governance to ensure that the metaverse becomes a force for good, benefiting individuals and communities around the globe.

This book is not a definitive guide to the metaverse, for the metaverse itself is an ever-evolving landscape. Instead, it is an exploration, a collection of insights, perspectives, and possibilities that inspire and provoke thought. It is an invitation for you, the reader, to embark on your own exploration, to envision the metaverse's potential and contribute to its evolution.

Whether you are a technology enthusiast, a business leader, an artist, an educator, or simply curious about the future, this book provides a roadmap to understanding the metaverse's vast potential and the opportunities and challenges that lie ahead. It is a call to action, urging us all to shape the metaverse in a way that aligns with our values, fosters human connection, and empowers individuals to thrive in this new digital landscape.

So, let us embark on this extraordinary journey into the metaverse together. Let us imagine, create, and collaborate, pushing the boundaries of what is possible. The metaverse awaits, and its future lies in our collective hands.

CONTENTS

Chapter 1. Introduction to MetaVerse

The term "metaverse" refers to a virtual reality-based universe that encompasses all virtual worlds, augmented reality, and the internet as a whole. It is often described as a collective virtual shared space where people can interact with each other and computer-generated environments in real-time. The concept of the metaverse gained significant attention and popularity in recent years, with discussions and developments focused on creating immersive and interconnected digital experiences.

The metaverse is envisioned as a seamless and immersive digital realm that goes beyond individual virtual reality games or applications. It allows users to navigate through various virtual environments, socialize with other users, engage in activities, and even conduct business transactions. It offers a blend of virtual reality, augmented reality, and mixed reality technologies to create a compelling and interactive digital universe.

Figure 1: shared virtual 3D world

The metaverse is the emerging 3-D-enabled digital space that uses virtual reality, augmented reality, and other advanced internet and semiconductor technology to allow people to have lifelike personal and business experiences online.

The metaverse is expected to have a wide range of applications across different domains. It has the potential to revolutionize entertainment, gaming, communication, education, commerce, and more. It could provide new ways for people to connect, collaborate, and share experiences, transcending geographical boundaries.

Several technology companies, including Facebook (now Meta), Microsoft, and various startups, have expressed their interest in developing and shaping the metaverse. They are investing in research, development, and infrastructure to make this vision a reality. However, it is important to note that the metaverse is still in its early stages, and the exact form and implementation of this concept are yet to be fully realized.

Figure 2: Interaction and Technologies In Metaverse

While the metaverse holds great promise for the future, it also raises questions and concerns regarding privacy, security, digital rights, and the potential for creating virtual monopolies. These issues need to be carefully addressed as the development of the metaverse progresses The metaverse represents a significant evolution in how we interact with digital technologies. It has the potential to reshape the way we live, work, and socialize, offering new possibilities for immersive and interconnected digital experiences.

1.1 Definition and Overview of the Metaverse

The metaverse is a term used to describe a virtual reality-based universe that encompasses a combination of physical reality, augmented reality, and virtual reality. It is essentially a collective digital space where users can interact with each other and computer-generated environments in real-time, blurring the lines between the physical and virtual worlds.

In the metaverse, users can navigate through various virtual environments, engage in social activities, interact with virtual objects, and even conduct business transactions. It is envisioned as a seamless and immersive digital realm that goes beyond individual applications or games, offering a unified and interconnected experience.

The Metaverse is an increasingly complex concept in the digital landscape, promising exceptional opportunities for billions of people via interconnected Web3 services and technology.

Mark Zuckerberg, CEO of leading immersive technology firm Meta, calls the Metaverse an "embodied internet". It's something user can access via VR or AR hardware. Meta debuted the Presence Platform at Connect 2021, which powers AR/MR Metaverse content using the Meta Quest Pro headset.

Research collected by Meta UK's Future of Work division highlighted how 81 percent of questioned individuals want to work in collaborative environments. The report claims that roughly 16 percent believe video calls help them feel present in meetings. A further 14 participants thought video conferencing led to greater collaboration with colleagues. Due to these figures, Meta believes companies should begin investing in XR headsets over laptops.

To go little deeper, the Metaverse offers a future where we can enjoy a more substantial overlap between our physical and digital lives. At a consumer level, immersive technology companies leverage extended reality (XR) tech, like the iPhone's LiDAR scanner, to display AR content.

Additionally, many opportunities have arisen for digital artists thanks to NFT and blockchain solutions, enabling content creators to monetize their work on Metaverse service. With the rise of inoperable Metaverse services, users can take their purchased digital goods, such as avatar clothing, and use them across different services.

The concept of the metaverse has gained significant attention and popularity due to advancements in technology and the increasing desire for immersive digital experiences. It has been portrayed in popular culture, such as books, movies, and video games, and has become a focal point for discussions among technologists, entrepreneurs, and futurists.

The metaverse holds great potential in various domains. In entertainment and gaming, it can offer deeply immersive and interactive experiences, allowing users to explore virtual worlds, play games, and engage with other players. In communication and socialization, it can provide new ways for people to connect, collaborate, and socialize regardless of physical distance. Additionally, it can transform education, training, and remote work by enabling virtual classrooms, simulations, and virtual collaboration spaces.

While the exact form and implementation of the metaverse are still evolving, several technology companies are investing in its development. Facebook (now Meta), Microsoft, and other major players are actively researching and creating technologies and platforms that aim to build the metaverse.

However, it is essential to consider the challenges and implications associated with the metaverse. Privacy, security, ethical concerns, digital rights, and potential monopolistic control are some of the issues that need to be carefully addressed as the metaverse evolves.

The metaverse represents a vision of a fully immersive and interconnected digital realm that combines virtual reality, augmented reality, and other technologies. It has the potential to revolutionize various aspects of our lives, offering new possibilities for communication, collaboration, entertainment, and more.

1.2 Significance and Impact of the Metaverse

The metaverse has the potential to bring about significant changes and impact across various domains. Here are some key areas where the metaverse can have a significant influence:

Communication and Socialization: The metaverse can revolutionize how people connect and interact with each other. It can offer immersive and engaging social experiences, enabling users to meet, socialize, collaborate, and share experiences in virtual environments. This can have a profound impact on long-distance relationships, remote work, and global collaboration.

Entertainment and Gaming: The metaverse can transform the entertainment and gaming industries by providing immersive and interactive experiences. It can offer new forms of storytelling, virtual concerts, live events, and multiplayer gaming on a massive scale. Users can explore vast virtual worlds, create personalized avatars, and engage in a wide range of activities.

Commerce and Business: The metaverse has the potential to revolutionize e-commerce and digital transactions. It can provide a platform for virtual marketplaces, enabling users to buy and sell virtual goods, assets, and services. Businesses can create virtual storefronts, showcase their products, and reach a global audience. The metaverse can also facilitate virtual conferences, meetings, and remote collaboration, transforming the way we work.

Education and Training: The metaverse can enhance education and training by creating immersive and interactive learning experiences. It can offer virtual classrooms, simulations, and personalized learning environments. Students can explore historical sites, conduct virtual experiments, and engage in collaborative learning with peers from around the world. Training programs can utilize the metaverse to simulate real-world scenarios and provide hands-on experiences.

Healthcare and Therapy: The metaverse has the potential to revolutionize healthcare and therapy. It can enable telemedicine and remote patient monitoring, allowing doctors to provide healthcare services from anywhere. Virtual reality can be used for pain management, exposure therapy, and rehabilitation. The metaverse can also create virtual support groups and therapy sessions, offering accessible and inclusive mental health resources.

Creativity and Self-expression: The metaverse can provide a platform for creative expression and artistic endeavors. Users can create and showcase their artwork, music, and virtual designs. It can offer new avenues for digital content creation, storytelling, and immersive experiences. The metaverse can democratize creativity by giving everyone the opportunity to participate and contribute to the digital world.

While the metaverse presents exciting opportunities, it also raises concerns and challenges. Privacy, security, digital rights, inclusivity, and the potential for virtual monopolies are some of the issues that need to be carefully addressed. As the metaverse continues to evolve, it will require collaboration, innovation, and ethical considerations to maximize its positive impact while mitigating any potential drawbacks.

Real-world METAVERSE Examples

Currently dozens of companies are working on Metaverse including tech giants like Meta, NVidia, Epic Games, Microsoft, and Apple. Currently there a few platforms that claim toa be Metaverse, but they are still in development phase and still lack some of the core features of a true Metaverse. Here are some of the closest Metaverse Examples:

Fortnite is a free-to-play battle royale game developed and published by Epic Games with over 350 million players. Fortnite is primarily a multiplayer shooting game that allows multiple people to connect and play and compete against each other in a shared space. Fortnite, the battle-royale-style action game published by Epic Games, sprang to notoriety in 2019. Functionally a virtual hub for social connection and attending live events, Fornite spans multiple platforms, including PC, mobile and several game consoles, offering an unforeseen degree of interoperability to users despite being in an industry that historically prefers to operate inside walled gardens. That interoperability, along with the way it allows wildly diverse IP to coexist in its game — you might see Iron Man fighting alongside Indiana Jones and LeBron James, for instance — is why Fortnite offers a glimpse into the possibilities of the metaverse.

Virtual Real Estate: We can now use the metaverse technology in order to enable the purchase and sale of virtual real estate through the use of cryptocurrencies. Virtual real estate is an important source of investments for an upcoming investor because more and more people are getting interested in the metaverse and NFTs.

Ready Player One: This film uses metaverse technology to showcase to the users the true capacity of the metaverse technology. The touch-sensitive gloves and virtual reality headset used in the film give us a slight glimpse into what the future of the Metaverse looks like.

Second Life: Second Life is one of the examples of a gaming metaverse, where the users have the ability to create their own digital avatars and characters to host their online open gaming world with the help of metaverse technology.

The Sandbox: The Sandbox is basically a virtual reality metaverse that allows users to experience, explore and play in a three-dimensional world. It also allows players to create their own digital avatars and characters to host their online open gaming world with the help of metaverse technology. Users can also buy some NFTs for the in-game purchases for customizing their characters.

Decentraland: A piece of virtual real estate property on Decentraland was auctioned off for a price of $2.4 million. Decentraland is one of the best metaverse examples to acknowledge the true potential of metaverse technology.

Illuvium: It is an open-world role-based game that uses the Ethereum cryptocurrency-based Blockchain network and it is expected to be released in 2022. Here, the users search for the collecting NFTs, which represent each Illuvial.

How Does the Metaverse Work?

In theory, the metaverse works by allowing an infinite number of people to synchronously connect together in real time in an always-on virtual environment that's immersive, three-dimensional and connects to our physical world in seamless ways.

In reality, it's a tricky technological feat to accomplish. Such a thing requires enormous amounts of computer processing and advancements made in smartphone, gaming device and VR and AR headset technology.

Plus, a single, interoperable metaverse — one that would let users carry their identities and digital collectibles across platforms owned by different companies — would require serious coordination and cooperation between various organizations.

Historically, companies (gaming companies especially) have been hesitant to allow their assets to be compatible with a competitor's ecosystem. Playing nicely with other platforms, the logic goes, would mean giving up some amount of control. But for a fully realized metaverse to come about, such cooperation will be necessary.

But what, exactly, is the metaverse? Where can it be found? Why does it matter? And more importantly, how can you and I get in?

In theory, the metaverse works by allowing an infinite number of people to synchronously connect together in real time in an always-on virtual environment that's immersive, three-dimensional and connects to our physical world in seamless ways.

In reality, it's a tricky technological feat to accomplish. Such a thing requires enormous amounts of computer processing and advancements made in smartphone, gaming device and VR and AR headset technology.

Plus, a single, interoperable metaverse — one that would let users carry their identities and digital collectibles across platforms owned by different companies — would require serious coordination and cooperation between various organizations.

Historically, companies (gaming companies especially) have been hesitant to allow their assets to be compatible with a competitor's ecosystem. Playing nicely with other platforms, the logic goes, would mean giving up some amount of control. But for a fully realized metaverse to come about, such cooperation will be necessary. People who want to participate in metaverse-like experiences have a number of options:

- Buy a virtual reality headset and join a social VR experience like Horizon Worlds, VRChat or Rec Room.
- Create a free account on a platform like Roblox, Fortnite or Minecraft, which you can experience on a PC, mobile device or gaming console.
- Check out ethereum-based virtual worlds like The Sandbox and Decentraland.

In the future, there may be a main hub that connects users to each part of the metaverse, like the forest in The Nightmare Before Christmas, with magical doors that allow anyone to move seamlessly in and out of discrete worlds.

However, there are several experts who may argue that we don't require any such headsets to enter the metaverse. We may be able to access the metaverse through smartphones, similar to how we access the internet. As of now, information about being able to access the metaverse is uncertain. As we gain more knowledge about the same, we may be able to clearly define a way of entering the metaverse.

How to access Metaverse?

There is no single way of accessing the metaverse at this point in time. Baggili, a cybersecurity expert, says that there are multiple platforms that offer VR, augmented reality, and extended reality. However, there is no single portal to use these. This has led to multiple tech companies offering different varieties of experiences, be it gaming, virtual workplaces, real estate, or shopping. Platforms such as Fortnite, Roblox, decentral, and Sandbox are a few such examples. These worlds can typically be accessed through a VR headset where users can navigate with the help of voice controllers, eye movements, or motion sensing controllers. This creates a feeling of physically being present in the virtual world.

To access the metaverse in action, we can look at popular multiplayer games such as Fortnite, Rec Room, or Horizon Worlds. The wider and newer applications of the metaverse that tech companies are experimenting with are building virtual stadiums to watch a football game, hosting concerts, or virtual shopping.

The next version of the internet is coming, and it's called the metaverse. Just ask the leader of the company formerly known as Facebook, which in 2021 rebranded itself as Meta after CEO Mark Zuckerberg announced the social networking platform has its sights set on becoming a "metaverse company."

1.3 Historical Development and Origins

The concept of the metaverse has its roots in science fiction literature and popular culture. The term "metaverse" was coined by Neal Stephenson in his 1992 science fiction novel "Snow Crash." In the book, the metaverse is depicted as a virtual reality-based successor to the internet, where users can interact with each other and with computer-generated environments.

Since the publication of "Snow Crash," the idea of the metaverse has captured the imagination of many, including technologists and entrepreneurs. It has served as a conceptual framework for envisioning a fully immersive and interconnected digital universe.

In the early 2000s, virtual worlds such as Second Life gained popularity and drew attention to the possibilities of creating virtual social spaces. While not fully realizing the concept of the metaverse, these virtual worlds provided a glimpse into the potential for virtual interactions and digital economies.

In recent years, advancements in technology and the growing interest in virtual reality, augmented reality, and mixed reality have sparked renewed discussions and developments around the metaverse. Companies like Facebook (now Meta) have made significant investments in virtual reality and have expressed their vision of building the metaverse.

The COVID-19 pandemic also played a role in accelerating the interest in the metaverse. With people seeking alternative ways to connect and socialize during lockdowns, virtual environments became more appealing. The pandemic highlighted the potential of the metaverse for remote collaboration, virtual events, and immersive experiences.

It is important to note that the development of the metaverse is still ongoing, and there is no universally accepted definition or specific implementation. The metaverse is a broad and evolving concept, shaped by the collective efforts of various technology companies, researchers, and developers.

While the origins of the metaverse can be traced back to science fiction and early virtual worlds, its current development is driven by technological advancements, entrepreneurial visions, and the growing demand for immersive digital experiences.

The term "metaverse" first appeared in author Neal Stephenson's 1992 science-fiction novel Snowcrash, which describes a future where millions of people use virtual avatars to participate in a cyberspace realm. This concept was further popularized in another sci-fi novel, Earnest Cline's 2011 Ready Player One, in which everyday people strap on VR headsets and log into a virtual world to live out their fantasies.

The metaverse also exists beyond literature: In 2003, the company Linden Lab launched Second Life. Considered to be one of the earliest real-life examples of a metaverse (or something close to it), Second Life isn't quite a game — there are no points or overarching objectives — but a simulated 3D environment where users can do practically anything. They can adopt new personas, cultivate hobbies, run businesses and create friendships with people from far-flung geographies.

Second Life proved to be a massive hit upon release, with around a million users signing up. Harvard University held classes in it, rapper Jay-Z threw a concert in it and Rolling Stone called it "the future of the Net." Eventually, though, enthusiasm for Second Life waned, and the platform's growth flattened. Still, its cultural impact signaled the possibility of a metaverse.

Why Is MetaVerse Relevant?

Metaverse has caught the attention of everyone in the computer, software, and tech industry. It is made possible by virtual and augmented reality technology and is referred to by many experts as the next version of the internet. Given the variety of its potential use cases, it is only a matter of time before the idea becomes a reality.

Starting with payments and ending with identification verification, everything has gone digital. Therefore, a virtual world like the metaverse has the potential to change how businesses and individuals view and use technology. Here, we go over a few of its potential applications.

4 key innovations make metaverse a strategic technology trend:

- Innovation No. 1: Web3, which is a new stack of technologies for the development of decentralized web applications that enable users to control their own identity and data. Web3 and metaverse complement each in a community or ecosystem where value in some form is exchanged between people or organizations — or a combination.

- Innovation No. 2: Spatial computing, which can be defined as a three-tiered technology stack through which users experience the intersection of the physical and digital worlds.

- Innovation No. 3: Digital twin of a person (DToP) not only mirrors a unique individual, but is also a near-real-time synchronized multipresence, with the ability to be present in multiple places at the same time in both digital and physical spaces.

- Innovation No. 4: Digital twin of a customer (DToC), a subset of DToP, is a dynamic virtual representation of a customer that simulates and learns to emulate and anticipate behavior. Customers can be individuals, personas, groups of people or machines.

1.4 Features of Metaverse

Immersive experiences: Metaverse enables users to have immersive experiences in a virtual world, where they can interact with other users and objects in real-time.

Customization: Users can customize their avatars and virtual spaces to reflect their personalities, preferences, and style.

Social interactions: Metaverse allows users to connect and socialize with other users worldwide in a virtual environment.

Shared experiences: Users can participate in shared experiences and activities, such as games, events, and virtual concerts.

Cross-platform support: Metaverse is accessible across different platforms and devices, such as mobile phones, tablets, and desktop computers.

Digital ownership: Users can own and trade digital assets, such as virtual real estate, virtual currency, and unique digital items.

Integration with the real world: Metaverse has the potential to integrate with the real world in various ways, such as virtual tourism, remote work, and e-commerce.

How to buy land in the metaverse?

The virtual estate is already a big business. Global businesses and superstars such as JP Morgan, Snoop Dog, PwC, and Samsung already have virtual lands intended to be developed for a variety of reasons. Less than a year ago, the average price for a plot of virtual land on Decentraland or Sandbox (metaverse platforms) – was around $1000, whereas today, that same plot costs around $13,000. But how exactly can we buy lanWeb3 vs. the Metaverse

The word metaverse is sometimes mentioned in parallel with another buzzy term — Web3. And while the two concepts share similarities — both cast a vision of the next-generation version of the internet — they are not identical and shouldn't be used interchangeably.

Web3 is a term used to describe a decentralized internet built on a blockchain foundation. Central to Web3's premise is that power over the internet will eventually swing away from a handful of tech giants and toward the many individual users and developers.

That said, none of Web3's core tenets run contrary to those of the metaverse. It's entirely possible that both visions will co-exist in the future.eum or SAND (a game version of the metaverse, the Sandbox) and MANA (connected to the Decentraland platform). When it comes to owning virtual land, these two platforms are currently the popularly known ones. They have well-known established companies and celebrities being part of their virtual worlds. Purchase land, it can be done directly on the platform, and any sales are recorded via transfer of NFTs. You will require a wallet that is capable of storing this, such as Metamask or Binance.

Apart from these platforms, you can buy virtual land on the metaverse from third-party resellers such as opensea.io or nonfungible.com. The future directly depends on the metaverse itself. Big corporations such as Facebook (now, meta) claim that the metaverse is the "next big thing." However, it is too soon to tell what the future would look like.

Web3 vs. the Metaverse

The word metaverse is sometimes mentioned in parallel with another buzzy term — Web3. And while the two concepts share similarities — both cast a vision of the next-generation version of the internet — they are not identical and shouldn't be used interchangeably.

Web3 is a term used to describe a decentralized internet built on a blockchain foundation. Central to Web3's premise is that power over the internet will eventually swing away from a handful of tech giants and toward the many individual users and developers.

That said, none of Web3's core tenets run contrary to those of the metaverse. It's entirely possible that both visions will co-exist in the future.

METAVERSE VS. THE INTERNET: WHAT'S THE DIFFERENCE?

The metaverse is a massive network constantly buzzing with activity where people remotely hang out with friends, create art, play games and shop — so how's that any different from the internet as we know it today?

Matthew Ball conceives of the metaverse not as something wholly separate from the internet, but an evolution of it — an embodied internet you are within, rather than have access to.

"The metaverse will not replace or fundamentally alter the internet's underlying architecture or protocol suite," Ball wrote in The Metaverse. "Instead, it will evolve to build on top of it in a way that will feel distinctive."

The similarities don't stop there: "The way the metaverse looks is very similar to how the internet emerged," Pim de Witte, co-founder and chief executive officer of Medal, a game-clip-sharing platform, told Built In.

De Witte conceives of the metaverse not as a single destination that everyone defaults to, but as a complex network consisting of browsers, indexes and destinations.

He explained it like this: Platforms such as Fortnite, Roblox and Minecraft are not in themselves metaverses, but destinations within the metaverse. There will be lots of these sorts of destinations, not unlike individual websites on the internet today. In other words, Fortnite is not a metaverse, in the same way that Facebook is not an internet. The two are both planets within a larger galaxy.

BLOCKCHAIN, WEB3 AND THE METAVERSE

The next frontier of the internet may very well be shaped by companies and projects related to blockchain, Web3 and the metaverse. As stated previously, these concepts are not at odds with one another. In fact, they may support and complement each other as we build toward a more equitable, inclusive, open and secure internet.

Two popular examples positioning themselves at the intersection of blockchain, Web3 and the metaverse are The Sandbox and Decentraland. Both offer immersive virtual worlds, as well as tools that allow users to build monetizable projects within those worlds. And unlike many tech companies commonly associated with the metaverse, The Sandbox and Decentraland are owned by their users and built on the Ethereum blockchain.

Cryptocurrency Made The Metaverse Possible

To enable commercial activities in the metaverse, the metaverse needs a system to support business transactions.

Trading goods and services in the virtual world have two challenges.

First, it needs a way to determine the value. Since any digital goods can be copied and replicated easily, the metaverse needs a way to identify the authenticity of the goods and the owners.

Just as you won't pay the same price for a faulty car or a fake Gucci knockoff, you likely don't want to pay the same price for any digital goods that are replicas of the original – even though they look the same.

Secondly, the metaverse needs a way to transact in the virtual world. It needs virtual currency.

This is where non-fungible tokens (NFT) and cryptocurrencies come to the rescue.

Both NFTs and cryptocurrencies are based on blockchain technology. While the technologies are quite complicated, their usages are quite simple to understand.

NFT acts as a certificate, like the title to a house. Even if the digital product itself can be replicated, the NFT cannot, and is always tied to the original. Hence, they're called non-fungible tokens.

Cryptocurrency is a natural fit with the metaverse. Since the metaverse is virtual, it is always active, self-sustaining, and creates incredible possibilities in business. And many of these possibilities hold a basis in cryptocurrency.

The advent of Bitcoin in 2009 kicked off the rising popularity of cryptocurrencies over the last decade. However, across the metaverse, Ethereum, which also supports NFTs, is the most popular cryptocurrency. It's also common for metaverse platforms to create their own versions of cryptocurrency. For example, the popular NFT art collection marketplace, Bored Ape Yacht Club, has its own cryptocurrency called ApeCoin.

1.5 Metaverse and the Challenges Ahead

Privacy: The Internet is not safe nowadays because most companies are misusing their user's information for targeting them with misleading ads. Hence, it is a big concern that these companies will use the Metaverse as an opportunity to earn more money as they could get a lot of information about the users which was not available before.

Discrimination: Metaverse will create more discrimination and prejudice in society as only a few people will be able to access it due to a lack of resources and money.

Women and Child Safety: Metaverse has caused huge damage to women and child safety issues in the past. Incidents have reported severe crimes against women and children in the Metaverse 3D virtual world. It is one of the most affecting concerns about the Metaverse.

User Addiction: People are more addicted to social media life. No one wants to live in real life and enjoy the people in personal relationships but people love to interact with each other online virtually. Metaverse will further degrade this and lead to more user addiction in the society with irresponsible lifestyle.

Law and Jurisdiction: Metaverse currently doesn't have any laws, rules, or jurisdictions enforced on it. When so many people will use the Metaverse, then there are high chances that crime will exist in the Metaverse and hence there aren't currently any laws that deal with the law and justice in the Metaverse.

Chapter 2. Understanding the Metaverse

The metaverse is a concept that refers to a collective virtual reality-based universe where people can interact with each other and computer-generated environments in real-time. It is an immersive and interconnected digital realm that goes beyond individual applications or games, creating a seamless and unified experience.

In the metaverse, users can navigate through various virtual environments, socialize with other users, engage in activities, and even conduct business transactions. It combines elements of virtual reality, augmented reality, and mixed reality to create a rich and interactive digital space.

The metaverse aims to transcend the limitations of the physical world and provide a new dimension of digital existence. It offers opportunities for communication, collaboration, entertainment, commerce, education, and more. It has the potential to transform various aspects of our lives and reshape how we interact with digital technologies.

Imagine stepping into a virtual world where you can meet and interact with friends and family from around the world, explore fantastical landscapes, play games, attend virtual concerts or events, create and sell virtual goods, attend virtual classes or training sessions, and even build and customize your own digital spaces. The possibilities within the metaverse are vast and diverse.

However, it is important to note that the metaverse is still a concept in development. There is no single platform or definitive implementation that represents the metaverse at this time. Various technology companies, including Facebook (Meta), Microsoft, and startups, are working on different aspects of the metaverse, such as creating virtual reality hardware, developing social platforms, and building immersive experiences.

The metaverse also raises important considerations and challenges. Privacy, security, digital rights, inclusivity, and the potential for creating virtual monopolies are some of the issues that need to be addressed as the metaverse evolves. It will require careful navigation and collaboration among various stakeholders to ensure that the metaverse is developed in an ethical and inclusive manner.

"Metaverse" the term was first coined in 1992 in Snow Crash, a Neil Stephenson sci-fi novel that propounds the onset of a dystopian digital reality where the physical world has become inhabitable and the only exit is through virtual reality.

The Metaverse, in its marketed form factor, is preserving its sanctity though. As described by Facebook, the Metaverse would be a unification of physical and virtual realities enabling peer-to-peer, lifelike interaction in digital work environments. Collaborations would imitate real-world experiences where AR and VR elements would combine to allow users to experience palpable conditions unbounded by the laws of physics (perhaps). Be it traveling, frolicking, working, or running you could theoretically do it all on the metaverse.

Many visionaries see the current version of the web as full of loose ends and irreparable chasms. The metaverse, in their view, could be the binding glue providing for interoperable, multi-sensory, and commercially viable conditions.

As we would discover in the later sections of this article, Facebook isn't the only flagbearer of the metaverse concept. In fact, these mixed reality environments are taking both centralized and distributed approaches towards mainstreaming with the help of AR VR software development.

In summary, the metaverse represents a vision of a fully immersive and interconnected digital universe where people can engage with each other and virtual environments. While it is still in development, it holds immense potential to transform how we communicate, collaborate, entertain ourselves, conduct business, and experience digital technologies.

2.1 Core Concepts and Characteristics

The metaverse is characterized by several core concepts and characteristics that define its nature and distinguish it from other digital environments. Here are some of the key concepts and characteristics associated with the metaverse:

Virtual Reality (VR) and Immersion: The metaverse relies heavily on virtual reality technology to create immersive and realistic experiences. Users can enter a virtual environment through VR headsets or other devices, which simulate a sense of presence and enable interaction with the virtual world.

Interconnectivity and Persistence: The metaverse is a network of interconnected virtual worlds and environments. It enables seamless movement and communication between different spaces, allowing users to explore and interact with various digital realms. Moreover, the metaverse maintains persistence, meaning that changes made by users persist over time, providing a sense of continuity and evolution.

Shared Experience and Social Interaction: One of the fundamental aspects of the metaverse is the ability for users to socialize and interact with each other in real-time. Users can meet, communicate, collaborate, and share experiences with other participants within the virtual environment, fostering a sense of community and connectedness.

User-Generated Content and Creativity: The metaverse empowers users to create and contribute their own content, adding to the richness and diversity of the virtual world. Users can create virtual objects, environments, avatars, and even entire virtual worlds. This user-generated content allows for personalization, customization, and creative expression within the metaverse.

Digital Economy and Commerce: The metaverse facilitates virtual commerce and digital economies. Users can buy, sell, and trade virtual goods, assets, and services within the virtual environment. Virtual currencies, marketplaces, and digital transactions enable economic activity and entrepreneurship within the metaverse.

Cross-Platform and Cross-Domain Integration: The metaverse is not limited to a single platform or domain. It aims to integrate various technologies, platforms, and applications, allowing users to access and interact with the metaverse from different devices and across different digital environments. This cross-platform and cross-domain integration promotes interoperability and broadens the reach of the metaverse.

Scalability and Openness: The metaverse is designed to accommodate a large number of users simultaneously. It should be scalable to support a massive user base and provide a seamless experience even with high levels of user activity. Additionally, the metaverse aims to be open, allowing developers and creators to contribute to its growth and development.

These core concepts and characteristics form the foundation of the metaverse, shaping its immersive nature, social dynamics, economic possibilities, and technological infrastructure. As the metaverse evolves, these concepts will continue to be refined and expanded upon, driving innovation and shaping the future of virtual experiences.

2.2 Technological Foundations

The metaverse relies on several technological foundations to create its immersive and interconnected digital environment. These technologies work together to enable the seamless virtual experiences and interactions within the metaverse. Here are some of the key technological foundations of the metaverse:

Virtual Reality (VR): Virtual reality is a crucial component of the metaverse, as it allows users to enter and interact with virtual environments in a highly immersive way. VR headsets, motion tracking, and haptic feedback systems provide a sense of presence and enable users to navigate and engage with the virtual world.

Augmented Reality (AR): Augmented reality enhances the metaverse by overlaying virtual elements onto the physical world. AR devices such as smart glasses or smartphones can blend digital information with the user's real environment, creating a mixed reality experience. This technology enables users to interact with virtual objects while still being aware of their physical surroundings.

Spatial Computing: Spatial computing technologies play a vital role in the metaverse by enabling the mapping of the physical and virtual worlds. These technologies use sensors, cameras, and algorithms to understand and interpret the user's physical environment, allowing for real-time tracking, positioning, and object recognition. This spatial awareness is essential for creating immersive and interactive virtual experiences.

Networking and Internet Infrastructure: The metaverse requires robust networking and internet infrastructure to facilitate real-time communication and interaction between users. High-speed internet connections, low-latency networks, and scalable server infrastructure are necessary to support the large-scale simultaneous presence of users and ensure smooth interactions within the metaverse.

Artificial Intelligence (AI): AI technologies contribute to the metaverse by enhancing virtual environments, enabling intelligent virtual characters and objects, and providing personalized experiences. AI algorithms can be used to create realistic virtual avatars, simulate natural language conversations, generate dynamic and responsive virtual environments, and personalize content based on user preferences.

Blockchain and Distributed Ledger Technology: Blockchain and distributed ledger technologies have the potential to support the digital economies within the metaverse. They can provide secure and transparent transactions, establish ownership and provenance of virtual assets, and facilitate decentralized governance and community-driven decision-making.

Content Creation Tools and Platforms: Content creation tools and platforms enable users to create, customize, and contribute their own content within the metaverse. These tools may include 3D modeling software, game engines, virtual world creation platforms, and user-friendly interfaces that allow individuals to express their creativity and contribute to the virtual ecosystem.

It is worth noting that the development and implementation of these technologies are ongoing, and the metaverse is still evolving. Technological advancements in areas such as AI, VR, AR, and networking infrastructure will continue to shape and enhance the metaverse, enabling more immersive, interactive, and seamless virtual experiences in the future.

2.3 Key Players and Platforms

Several key players and platforms are actively involved in the development and exploration of the metaverse. These companies and platforms are driving innovation, creating technologies, and building virtual environments to bring the concept of the metaverse closer to reality. Here are some of the notable key players and platforms in the metaverse space:

Meta (formerly Facebook): Meta, previously known as Facebook, is one of the major players in the metaverse arena. With its focus on virtual reality and augmented reality technologies, Meta aims to build a connected and immersive metaverse experience. The company is developing hardware like Oculus VR headsets and software platforms like Horizon Workrooms and Facebook Horizon.

Microsoft: Microsoft is actively involved in the metaverse space through its Mixed Reality platform and services. Their flagship product, Microsoft HoloLens, is an augmented reality headset that enables users to interact with holographic content in the physical world. Microsoft is also working on Mesh, a platform that aims to enable shared and collaborative experiences across devices and platforms.

Epic Games: Epic Games, the creator of the popular game Fortnite, is positioning itself as a significant player in the metaverse realm. The company is investing heavily in building the Epic Games Store and Unreal Engine, a powerful game development engine that enables the creation of immersive virtual experiences. Epic Games has also acquired companies like SuperAwesome and Capturing Reality to expand its metaverse capabilities.

Roblox: Roblox is a user-generated content platform that allows users to create and share their own virtual worlds and games. It has gained significant popularity, especially among younger audiences, and has millions of active users. Roblox provides a framework for developers to build and monetize their virtual experiences, making it a notable player in the metaverse landscape.

Decentraland: Decentraland is a blockchain-based virtual world that operates on the Ethereum network. It enables users to buy, sell, and trade virtual land and assets using non-fungible tokens (NFTs). Decentraland allows users to create and monetize their virtual experiences, providing a decentralized and user-driven metaverse environment.

Spatial.io: Spatial.io is a platform that focuses on collaborative virtual reality experiences. It allows users to meet and interact with others in shared virtual spaces, enabling remote collaboration, meetings, and presentations. Spatial.io emphasizes the social and collaborative aspects of the metaverse, providing tools for communication and interaction in a virtual environment.

Other Companies: In addition to the key players mentioned above, numerous other companies are involved in the metaverse space. This includes companies like Unity Technologies, Magic Leap, HTC, NVIDIA, Apple, and many startups that are exploring various aspects of the metaverse, such as virtual reality hardware, content creation tools, social platforms, and virtual marketplaces.

It's important to note that the metaverse ecosystem is still evolving, and the landscape may change over time. New players may emerge, and existing players may evolve their strategies and offerings. The competition and collaboration among these key players and platforms will shape the future development and realization of the metaverse concept.

Chapter 3. Metaverse Environments

Metaverse environments refer to the virtual spaces or worlds within the metaverse where users can explore, interact, and engage with the digital environment and other participants. These environments are designed to be immersive, interactive, and interconnected, providing users with a sense of presence and allowing them to navigate and experience the metaverse. Here are some common types of metaverse environments:

Virtual Worlds: Virtual worlds are immersive digital environments that simulate a three-dimensional space where users can interact with each other and the virtual surroundings. These worlds can range from realistic representations of physical locations to entirely fantastical and imaginative realms. Users can explore these virtual worlds, engage in activities, and interact with other participants.

Social Platforms: Social platforms within the metaverse focus on facilitating social interactions and connections. They provide virtual spaces where users can meet, communicate, and socialize with each other. These platforms often incorporate features like avatars, chat systems, voice chat, and virtual hangout spaces to enable socialization within the metaverse.

Gaming Environments: Gaming environments are a prominent part of the metaverse, offering interactive and immersive gameplay experiences. These environments can include massive multiplayer online games (MMOs), virtual reality games, augmented reality games, and other interactive gaming experiences within the metaverse. Users can engage in multiplayer gameplay, complete quests, and compete or cooperate with other players.

Creative Spaces: Metaverse environments also include spaces dedicated to creativity and self-expression. These spaces allow users to create and share their own digital content, such as artwork, music, virtual designs, and experiences. Users can showcase their creations, collaborate with others on creative projects, and participate in virtual events centered around art and creativity.

Virtual Marketplaces: Virtual marketplaces within the metaverse provide spaces for users to buy, sell, and trade virtual goods, assets, and services. These marketplaces enable users to create and monetize their virtual creations, such as virtual land, virtual fashion, virtual accessories, and more. Users can engage in economic activities, establish virtual businesses, and participate in a digital economy within the metaverse.

Educational and Training Environments: Metaverse environments also extend to education and training. Virtual classrooms, training simulations, and educational experiences can be created within the metaverse. These environments provide interactive and immersive learning experiences, allowing users to access educational content, collaborate with peers, and participate in virtual training programs.

It's important to note that the metaverse is an evolving concept, and the range of environments and their features may expand and diversify over time. These environments aim to provide users with diverse experiences, fostering social interactions, entertainment, creativity, learning, and economic opportunities within the metaverse.

3.1 Social Platforms in the Metaverse

Social platforms play a crucial role in the metaverse, facilitating social interactions, communication, and community building within the virtual environment. These platforms aim to recreate social experiences in a digital space and enable users to connect with each other, form relationships, and engage in shared activities. Here are some notable social platforms in the metaverse:

Facebook Horizon: Developed by Meta (formerly Facebook), Facebook Horizon is a social VR platform that allows users to create and customize their avatars, explore virtual worlds, and interact with other users in real-time. It offers various activities such as games, events, and creative tools, enabling socialization and community building within the metaverse.

VRChat: VRChat is a virtual reality social platform where users can create and customize their avatars, explore user-generated virtual worlds, and engage in real-time conversations with others. It emphasizes user-generated content and community-driven experiences, providing a space for social interaction, virtual events, and creative expression.

Rec Room: Rec Room is a social platform and virtual reality game that enables users to meet and play games together. It offers a wide range of activities and experiences, including multiplayer games, virtual events, and customizable spaces for social gatherings. Rec Room focuses on fostering social connections and collaborative gameplay within the metaverse.

AltspaceVR: AltspaceVR is a social platform designed for virtual reality where users can meet, interact, and attend virtual events. It offers features like customizable avatars, real-time voice chat, and the ability to host and join virtual gatherings, presentations, and performances. AltspaceVR aims to create a social space that replicates real-life social interactions and experiences.

Sansar: Sansar is a virtual social platform that allows users to create, share, and monetize their own virtual experiences. It offers customizable avatars, virtual spaces, and tools for building interactive environments. Sansar focuses on socialization, creativity, and immersive experiences within the metaverse.

Somnium Space: Somnium Space is a blockchain-based social virtual reality platform that offers a persistent virtual world. Users can explore, build, and monetize their virtual land, participate in virtual events, and interact with other users. Somnium Space emphasizes a user-driven economy and social interactions within the metaverse.

These are just a few examples of social platforms in the metaverse, and the landscape is continuously evolving as more companies and developers enter the space. These platforms aim to create immersive and interactive social experiences, allowing users to connect, collaborate, and engage with others in the virtual realm.

3.2 Gaming Worlds and Virtual Realms

Gaming worlds and virtual realms play a significant role in the metaverse, providing immersive and interactive gaming experiences within the virtual environment. These virtual spaces are designed specifically for gaming purposes and offer a wide range of gameplay mechanics, challenges, and social interactions. Here are some notable gaming worlds and virtual realms in the metaverse:

Fortnite: Fortnite is a massively popular online game developed by Epic Games. It features a large virtual world where players can engage in battle royale-style gameplay, building structures, and competing against other players. Fortnite has evolved into a social platform, hosting virtual events, concerts, and in-game collaborations with various brands and artists.

Minecraft: Minecraft is a sandbox-style game that allows players to create and explore virtual worlds made up of blocks. It offers both single-player and multiplayer modes, where players can build structures, mine resources, and engage in various activities. Minecraft has a strong community and supports user-generated content, making it a versatile and creative gaming world within the metaverse.

Roblox: Roblox is a user-generated content platform that offers a vast array of virtual worlds and games created by its users. It provides tools and resources for developers to create their own games, which can be played by millions of players. Roblox encompasses a wide range of genres, including role-playing games, simulations, and social experiences, making it a highly diverse gaming realm within the metaverse.

Second Life: Second Life is a virtual world that offers a user-driven economy and social interactions. It allows users to create and customize their avatars, build virtual properties, and engage in various activities like socializing, shopping, and attending virtual events. Second Life combines gaming elements with socialization and creativity, offering a unique gaming realm within the metaverse.

Decentraland: Decentraland is a blockchain-based virtual world where users can own and monetize virtual land and assets using non-fungible tokens (NFTs). It provides a platform for users to create and explore immersive experiences, including games, art installations, virtual marketplaces, and social interactions. Decentraland allows for user-driven content creation and economic opportunities within the gaming realm of the metaverse.

PlayStation Home: Although discontinued in 2015, PlayStation Home was a virtual world developed by Sony for PlayStation consoles. It provided a shared social space where players could meet, interact, and customize their avatars. PlayStation Home featured virtual spaces representing real-life locations, as well as games and activities for social engagement.

These gaming worlds and virtual realms offer a range of experiences, from competitive multiplayer games to creative sandboxes and social spaces. They provide opportunities for players to connect, collaborate, and explore within the metaverse, blurring the lines between gaming and social interaction.

3.3 Virtual Marketplaces and E-Commerce

Virtual marketplaces and e-commerce platforms play a vital role in the metaverse, enabling users to buy, sell, and trade virtual goods, assets, and services within the virtual environment. These platforms provide a digital marketplace where users can engage in economic activities, establish virtual businesses, and participate in a thriving virtual economy. Here are some aspects of virtual marketplaces and e-commerce in the metaverse:

Virtual Goods and Assets: Virtual marketplaces offer a wide range of virtual goods and assets for users to buy and sell. These can include virtual clothing, accessories, avatars, virtual land, virtual vehicles, in-game items, and more. Users can customize their virtual presence or enhance their gaming experiences by purchasing or trading these virtual assets.

Non-Fungible Tokens (NFTs): Non-Fungible Tokens have gained significant popularity in the metaverse as a way to establish ownership and value for digital assets. NFTs are unique digital tokens that represent ownership of a specific item or piece of content. Virtual marketplaces utilize NFTs to enable the trading and ownership of virtual assets, providing a secure and transparent way for users to buy, sell, and collect digital items.

Digital Art and Collectibles: Virtual marketplaces in the metaverse often showcase digital art and collectibles created by artists and creators. These platforms allow artists to sell their digital artworks or limited edition collectibles as NFTs, providing a new avenue for artists to monetize their creations. Users can purchase and collect digital art pieces, fostering a market for digital art within the metaverse.

Virtual Real Estate: Virtual marketplaces also offer virtual land and properties for users to buy and sell. Users can acquire virtual land within the metaverse, which they can develop, monetize, and sell to other users. Virtual real estate transactions within the metaverse can involve the purchase of virtual plots, virtual buildings, or even entire virtual regions.

In-Game Economies: Many virtual marketplaces exist within gaming worlds in the metaverse. These platforms allow players to buy, sell, and trade in-game items, currencies, and resources. In-game economies provide players with opportunities to acquire rare or valuable items, trade with other players, and participate in virtual commerce.

Digital Services and Experiences: Virtual marketplaces can also facilitate the buying and selling of digital services and experiences within the metaverse. This may include services like virtual event organization, virtual event ticketing, virtual tours, virtual performances, and more. Users can engage in or provide services within the metaverse, creating new avenues for business and entrepreneurship.

Blockchain and Cryptocurrency Integration: Virtual marketplaces in the metaverse often leverage blockchain technology and cryptocurrencies for secure transactions and ownership verification. Blockchain technology provides transparency, decentralization, and immutability, while cryptocurrencies can serve as a medium of exchange within the virtual economy.

These virtual marketplaces and e-commerce platforms contribute to the growth of the metaverse by enabling economic activities, fostering entrepreneurship, and providing users with opportunities to monetize their virtual presence and creations. They form the foundation of the virtual economy, allowing users to participate in a digital marketplace within the metaverse.

3.4 Collaborative Workspaces

Collaborative workspaces in the metaverse refer to virtual environments designed to facilitate remote collaboration, communication, and productivity among individuals and teams. These workspaces leverage the capabilities of the metaverse to provide interactive and immersive platforms for remote work, virtual meetings, and collaborative projects. Here are some examples of collaborative workspaces in the metaverse:

Spatial: Spatial is a collaborative workspace in the metaverse that enables teams to work together in a virtual environment. It combines virtual reality (VR) and augmented reality (AR) technologies to create an immersive workspace where users can collaborate on projects, brainstorm ideas, and hold virtual meetings. Spatial allows users to import documents, images, and 3D models, making it easy to work on shared content in a virtual space.

Mozilla Hubs: Mozilla Hubs is an open-source platform that allows users to create and customize virtual spaces for collaboration. It provides a virtual meeting space where users can gather, communicate, and collaborate using avatars. Mozilla Hubs supports features like audio and video chat, screen sharing, and the ability to import and manipulate media files. It is accessible across different devices, including desktops, VR headsets, and mobile devices.

Microsoft Mesh: Microsoft Mesh is a platform that enables collaborative workspaces in mixed reality, combining virtual reality and augmented reality experiences. It allows users to meet and collaborate in a shared virtual space using avatars, holograms, and 3D models. Microsoft Mesh integrates with various Microsoft applications and services, providing seamless integration with productivity tools like Microsoft 365.

Engage: Engage is a virtual reality collaboration platform that offers immersive virtual spaces for remote teams. It provides customizable meeting rooms, training environments, and interactive presentation spaces. Engage supports features such as real-time voice chat, multimedia sharing, whiteboarding, and interactive 3D objects. It aims to enhance remote collaboration and provide a virtual workspace for a range of professional applications.

Virbela: Virbela is a virtual world platform that offers a collaborative workspace for remote teams. It provides customizable virtual office spaces where users can work, meet, and interact with each other. Virbela supports features like spatial audio, screen sharing, presentation tools, and customizable avatars. It is designed to foster a sense of presence and enable natural interactions within the virtual workspace.

NeosVR: NeosVR is a collaborative virtual reality platform that allows users to create, share, and collaborate on projects within a shared virtual space. It offers a wide range of creative tools and allows users to build their own virtual environments, import 3D assets, and collaborate on interactive projects. NeosVR supports real-time collaboration, scripting, and advanced customization options.

These collaborative workspaces in the metaverse aim to bridge the gap between physical and virtual work environments, enabling remote teams to collaborate effectively and engage in productive work activities. They leverage the immersive and interactive nature of the metaverse to provide a rich and engaging collaborative experience.

Chapter 4. Metaverse Technologies

Metaverse technologies encompass a variety of technologies that enable the creation, operation, and interaction within the metaverse. These technologies are essential for building virtual environments, facilitating user interactions, and supporting the infrastructure required for the metaverse to function. Here are some key technologies commonly associated with the metaverse:

Virtual Reality (VR): Virtual reality technology allows users to immerse themselves in a computer-generated virtual environment. VR headsets, controllers, and sensors provide a sense of presence and enable users to interact with the virtual world through natural movements. VR technology enhances the immersive experience within the metaverse, creating a sense of being physically present in the virtual environment.

Augmented Reality (AR): Augmented reality technology overlays virtual content onto the real world, enhancing the user's perception of their physical surroundings. AR devices, such as smart glasses or mobile devices, enable users to see and interact with virtual objects and information in real-time. AR technology can be used in the metaverse to blend virtual and physical elements, creating mixed reality experiences.

3D Graphics and Modeling: 3D graphics and modeling technologies are crucial for creating realistic and visually appealing virtual environments within the metaverse. These technologies involve the creation and manipulation of 3D models, textures, lighting, and animations to build immersive digital spaces. High-quality 3D graphics and modeling contribute to the realism and aesthetic appeal of the metaverse.

Spatial Computing: Spatial computing technologies enable the understanding and mapping of physical space, allowing virtual objects and interactions to be accurately positioned and integrated into the real world. Spatial computing combines various technologies such as computer vision, depth sensing, and mapping to create a seamless integration of virtual and physical elements in the metaverse.

Networking and Cloud Infrastructure: Networking and cloud infrastructure technologies are crucial for supporting the connectivity and scalability of the metaverse. These technologies enable users from different locations to interact within the same virtual environment, facilitate real-time communication and synchronization, and ensure the efficient delivery of content and data. Robust networking and cloud infrastructure are necessary to support the collaborative and interactive nature of the metaverse.

Blockchain and Cryptocurrencies: Blockchain technology and cryptocurrencies are increasingly integrated into the metaverse to support secure transactions, ownership verification, and digital asset management. Blockchain provides a decentralized and transparent ledger that can be used to authenticate and track ownership of virtual assets, while cryptocurrencies serve as a medium of exchange within the virtual economy of the metaverse.

Artificial Intelligence (AI): Artificial intelligence technologies can enhance the metaverse by enabling intelligent virtual characters, automated behaviors, and personalized experiences. AI algorithms can be used to create responsive and interactive virtual entities, simulate realistic behaviors, and provide personalized recommendations and assistance to users within the metaverse.

These technologies, among others, work together to create the infrastructure and capabilities needed to build and operate the metaverse. They enable the immersive and interactive experiences within the virtual environment, supporting communication, collaboration, and the seamless integration of virtual and physical elements.

4.1 7 Layers of Metaverse Technology

Physical infrastructure: This layer includes the hardware and networking infrastructure that supports the Metaverse, such as servers, data centers, and high-speed internet connections.

Metaverse architecture: This layer includes the software and protocols that enable

communication and interoperability between different virtual worlds and platforms.

User interface: This layer includes the tools and interfaces that allow users to navigate and interact with the Metaverse, such as virtual reality headsets, controllers, and haptic feedback devices.

Identity and authentication: This layer includes the systems that manage user identities, authentication, and access control within the Metaverse.

Digital assets and economies: This layer includes the systems that enable the creation, ownership, and trade of digital assets within the Metaverse, such as virtual real estate, avatars, and virtual currency.

Social interactions and communities: This layer includes the systems that support social interactions and communities within the Metaverse, such as chat rooms, forums, and social media.

Governance and regulations: This layer includes the rules, regulations, and governance structures that guide and regulate the use of the Metaverse, such as terms of service, intellectual property rights, and privacy policies.

4.2 Virtual Reality (VR) and Augmented Reality (AR)

Virtual Reality (VR) and Augmented Reality (AR) are key technologies that play a significant role in the metaverse, providing immersive and interactive experiences for users. While both VR and AR have distinct characteristics and applications, they contribute to the overall metaverse experience in different ways:

Virtual Reality (VR):

Virtual Reality refers to the technology that creates a completely immersive and artificial digital environment, effectively transporting users into a virtual world. VR headsets, such as Oculus Rift or HTC Vive, cover the user's field of view, blocking out the physical surroundings and replacing them with a virtual environment. Within the metaverse, VR enables users to:

Engage in Immersive Experiences: VR allows users to feel present in the virtual environment, with the ability to interact with objects and surroundings. This immersion enhances the sense of being within the metaverse and facilitates a more engaging and realistic experience.

Explore Virtual Worlds: VR technology enables users to explore and navigate virtual worlds within the metaverse, moving and interacting with objects and other users in a three-dimensional space. This freedom of movement and interaction enhances the sense of presence and exploration within the metaverse.

Collaborate and Interact: VR facilitates social interactions within the metaverse, allowing users to meet, communicate, and collaborate in virtual spaces. Users can participate in virtual meetings, attend events, play games, and engage in shared activities, creating a sense of presence and togetherness despite physical distances.

Augmented Reality (AR):

Augmented Reality enhances the user's real-world environment by overlaying virtual content and information. AR technology, typically accessed through smartphones, tablets, or smart glasses, allows users to view both the physical world and virtual elements simultaneously. In the metaverse, AR enables users to:

Blend Virtual and Physical Realities: AR technology seamlessly integrates virtual elements into the user's real-world environment, enhancing the perception of the physical surroundings. This integration can include virtual objects, information, or interactive elements that coexist with the physical world.

Provide Contextual Information: AR overlays relevant information and data onto the user's field of view, providing real-time context and enhancing understanding. In the metaverse, AR can offer contextual information about virtual objects, people, or events, enriching the user's experience and providing additional details.

Enable Mixed Reality Experiences: AR can also create mixed reality experiences within the metaverse, where virtual and physical elements interact in real-time. Users can, for example, play virtual games in their living room, create virtual art on physical surfaces, or attend virtual events overlaid onto physical venues.

Both VR and AR technologies contribute to the metaverse by providing immersive, interactive, and spatially aware experiences. While VR offers a fully virtual and immersive environment, AR enhances the real world with virtual elements. Together, they create a dynamic and engaging metaverse where users can explore, communicate, collaborate, and interact within virtual spaces and with virtual entities.

4.3 Artificial Intelligence (AI) and Machine Learning (ML)

Artificial Intelligence (AI) and Machine Learning (ML) are integral technologies in the metaverse, enhancing the user experience, enabling intelligent interactions, and powering various functionalities. Here's how AI and ML contribute to the metaverse:

Intelligent Virtual Characters: AI and ML algorithms are used to create intelligent virtual characters within the metaverse. These characters can exhibit lifelike behaviors, respond to user interactions, and engage in realistic conversations. AI enables virtual characters to understand and interpret user inputs, adapt their responses, and provide personalized experiences, enhancing the sense of immersion and realism.

Natural Language Processing (NLP): NLP is an AI technique that enables computers to understand and process human language. In the metaverse, NLP algorithms power voice recognition, speech synthesis, and natural language understanding, allowing users to communicate with virtual entities using voice commands or text inputs. NLP facilitates natural and intuitive interactions, enabling users to have conversations, ask questions, and receive contextual responses within the metaverse.

Personalization and Recommendation Systems: AI and ML algorithms analyze user data and behavior to provide personalized experiences within the metaverse. These algorithms learn user preferences, interests, and habits, and use that information to recommend relevant content, events, or virtual experiences. Personalization enhances user engagement and satisfaction, tailoring the metaverse experience to individual needs and preferences.

Computer Vision: Computer vision algorithms enable the recognition and understanding of visual content within the metaverse. These algorithms can identify objects, detect gestures and facial expressions, and track user movements. Computer vision powers augmented reality applications, allowing virtual objects to be placed and interacted with in the real world. It also facilitates user tracking and avatar customization within virtual reality environments.

Intelligent Automation: AI and ML technologies can automate repetitive or complex tasks within the metaverse. For example, AI-powered bots can assist users in navigating virtual spaces, provide customer support, or perform administrative tasks. Intelligent automation frees up user time and enhances productivity within the metaverse, allowing users to focus on more meaningful interactions and experiences.

Content Generation and Adaptation: AI and ML algorithms can generate or adapt content within the metaverse. This includes generating virtual environments, landscapes, or objects procedurally, based on predefined rules or user preferences. AI can also adapt existing content, such as images, videos, or 3D models, to fit specific requirements or constraints within the metaverse.

Analytics and Insights: AI and ML techniques can be applied to analyze user behavior, interactions, and preferences within the metaverse. By analyzing data generated by users, AI algorithms can provide valuable insights into user engagement, trends, and patterns. These insights help developers and platform providers optimize the metaverse experience, make informed decisions, and deliver personalized content to users.

AI and ML technologies in the metaverse are continuously evolving, driving advancements in virtual intelligence, user interaction, and content creation. They enhance the metaverse experience by enabling intelligent virtual entities, personalizing interactions, automating tasks, and providing valuable insights based on user data.

4.4 Blockchain and Cryptocurrencies

Blockchain technology and cryptocurrencies play significant roles in the metaverse, providing decentralized and secure infrastructure, facilitating virtual economies, and enabling ownership and exchange of digital assets. Here's how blockchain and cryptocurrencies are utilized in the metaverse:

Decentralized Infrastructure: Blockchain technology provides a decentralized and distributed infrastructure for the metaverse. By using a network of computers (nodes) that validate and record transactions in a transparent and immutable manner, blockchain ensures the integrity and security of metaverse operations. This decentralized nature makes the metaverse resistant to censorship, fraud, and central points of failure.

Digital Asset Ownership: Blockchain enables the concept of digital asset ownership and provenance within the metaverse. Non-Fungible Tokens (NFTs), which are unique digital assets, are often used to represent virtual land, virtual objects, artwork, collectibles, and more. NFTs are created, bought, sold, and traded on blockchain platforms, allowing users to establish ownership and transfer digital assets securely and transparently.

Virtual Economies: Cryptocurrencies, such as Ethereum (ETH) or specialized in-game tokens, are used within the metaverse to create virtual economies. Users can earn, purchase, and spend these cryptocurrencies or tokens to buy virtual goods, services, or experiences. Cryptocurrencies provide a common medium of exchange within the metaverse, enabling economic transactions and creating opportunities for virtual entrepreneurship and commerce.

Secure Transactions: Blockchain technology ensures secure transactions within the metaverse. The use of smart contracts, self-executing contracts with predefined rules encoded on the blockchain, enables automated and tamper-proof transactions. Smart contracts facilitate secure peer-to-peer exchanges, escrow services, royalties, and revenue sharing models, enhancing trust and eliminating the need for intermediaries in the metaverse.

Authenticity and Verification: Blockchain technology can verify the authenticity and provenance of virtual assets within the metaverse. By recording the ownership history and transaction details of digital assets on the blockchain, users can verify the authenticity and ownership of virtual items, preventing counterfeiting or unauthorized replication. This enhances the value and trustworthiness of digital assets in the metaverse.

User Governance and Participation: Blockchain-based systems enable user governance and participation in the development and evolution of the metaverse. Decentralized autonomous organizations (DAOs) are created on the blockchain to allow community members to collectively make decisions and govern aspects of the metaverse. Token holders can participate in voting, proposals, and decision-making processes, shaping the metaverse according to the community's interests and values.

Interoperability and Cross-Platform Transactions: Blockchain technology facilitates interoperability and cross-platform transactions within the metaverse. Different virtual worlds, platforms, and applications can utilize blockchain standards and protocols to enable the transfer of digital assets across different environments. This interoperability allows users to bring their virtual assets and identities from one metaverse to another, expanding their experiences and possibilities.

Overall, blockchain technology and cryptocurrencies provide a robust and transparent framework for the metaverse, enabling secure transactions, establishing digital asset ownership, fostering virtual economies, and empowering users through decentralized governance. They create new opportunities for virtual entrepreneurship, creativity, and collaboration within the metaverse ecosystem.

4.5 Cloud Computing and Edge Computing

Cloud computing and edge computing are both essential technologies that contribute to the infrastructure and functionality of the metaverse. They play complementary roles in providing computing resources, storage, and network capabilities to support the metaverse experience. Here's an overview of cloud computing and edge computing in the metaverse:

Cloud Computing:

Cloud computing refers to the delivery of computing resources, including virtual machines, storage, and software services, over the internet. In the context of the metaverse, cloud computing offers several benefits:

Scalability: Cloud computing provides virtually unlimited scalability, allowing the metaverse to handle a large number of concurrent users, data processing, and content delivery. Cloud providers can dynamically allocate resources based on demand, ensuring optimal performance and responsiveness.

Storage and Processing Power: Cloud computing offers extensive storage and processing capabilities, enabling the storage and retrieval of large amounts of data in the metaverse. This is crucial for hosting virtual environments, user-generated content, and assets within the metaverse ecosystem.

Collaboration and Communication: Cloud-based collaboration tools and communication platforms facilitate real-time interactions and enable users to collaborate within the metaverse. Cloud-based services can handle voice chat, video conferencing, and real-time data synchronization, fostering teamwork and social interactions.

Content Delivery: Cloud-based content delivery networks (CDNs) help distribute content, such as virtual assets, images, videos, and updates, efficiently across different geographical locations. CDNs reduce latency and ensure fast and reliable content delivery to users, improving the overall metaverse experience.

Edge Computing:

Edge computing brings computing resources closer to the end-user, reducing latency and enhancing real-time interactions. In the metaverse, edge computing offers the following advantages:

Low Latency: Edge computing reduces latency by processing and delivering data closer to the user, minimizing the delay between user actions and the corresponding response in the metaverse. This is particularly important for real-time interactions, multiplayer gaming, and virtual experiences that require immediate feedback.

Edge Analytics: Edge computing enables real-time data analysis and processing at the network edge, allowing for faster insights and decision-making within the metaverse. It supports AI-powered features, object recognition, gesture tracking, and other interactive functionalities that require quick response times.

Bandwidth Optimization: By performing processing tasks at the network edge, edge computing reduces the amount of data that needs to be transmitted to the cloud, optimizing bandwidth usage. This is particularly beneficial in scenarios where the metaverse involves massive amounts of data or requires real-time interactions without overwhelming the network infrastructure.

Offline Capabilities: Edge computing can provide limited offline capabilities within the metaverse, allowing users to access certain features or content even when the internet connection is unreliable or unavailable. This is useful in scenarios where continuous connectivity is not guaranteed, such as remote areas or crowded environments.

In the metaverse, a combination of cloud computing and edge computing can be leveraged to optimize performance, scalability, and real-time interactions. While cloud computing provides the necessary backend infrastructure, storage, and processing power, edge computing brings the metaverse closer to the end-users, reducing latency and enabling more responsive experiences. The balance between cloud computing and edge computing depends on the specific requirements of the metaverse application and the desired user experience.

4.6 Internet of Things (IoT) and Sensor Networks

The Internet of Things (IoT) and sensor networks play a crucial role in the metaverse, enabling connectivity, data collection, and interaction with the physical world. They extend the metaverse experience beyond virtual environments, incorporating real-world data and interactions. Here's how IoT and sensor networks contribute to the metaverse:

Real-World Data Integration: IoT devices and sensor networks collect real-time data from physical environments and objects, which can be integrated into the metaverse. This data includes environmental conditions, location information, biometric data, and more. By incorporating real-world data, the metaverse becomes more contextually aware, allowing virtual experiences to react and adapt to real-world events.

Physical Object Interaction: IoT devices and sensors enable users to interact with physical objects and environments within the metaverse. For example, smart home devices, wearables, or IoT-enabled objects can be connected to the metaverse, allowing users to control and monitor them virtually. This integration creates seamless interactions between the virtual and physical worlds, enhancing the user experience.

Spatial Mapping and Localization: Sensor networks and IoT devices can be utilized for spatial mapping and localization within the metaverse. By leveraging technologies such as GPS, indoor positioning systems, or beacons, users' positions can be tracked accurately in virtual environments. This enables precise placement of virtual objects, facilitates navigation, and supports multiplayer interactions within the metaverse.

Enhanced Immersion and Realism: IoT and sensor networks contribute to the immersive and realistic nature of the metaverse by capturing and integrating real-world sensory data. For example, ambient lighting, temperature, or sound can be synchronized between the physical environment and the virtual world, creating a more engaging and immersive experience.

Environmental Interactions and Simulations: IoT devices and sensor networks enable environmental interactions and simulations within the metaverse. For instance, environmental sensors can capture real-time weather conditions, and these data can be used to simulate weather effects within virtual environments. Similarly, IoT-enabled objects or infrastructures can react to user interactions, creating dynamic and responsive virtual experiences.

User Tracking and Behavioral Analytics: Sensor networks and IoT devices can track user behavior and movements within the metaverse. This data can be leveraged to analyze user interactions, preferences, and engagement patterns. By understanding user behavior, developers can personalize experiences, optimize content delivery, and improve the overall metaverse ecosystem.

Extended Reality (XR) Integration: IoT devices and sensor networks can be integrated with Extended Reality (XR) technologies, such as Augmented Reality (AR) and Virtual Reality (VR), within the metaverse. For example, IoT-enabled wearables or haptic devices can provide tactile feedback, enhancing the immersion and realism of VR experiences. Similarly, AR applications can utilize real-time sensor data to overlay virtual content onto the physical world.

By integrating IoT and sensor networks into the metaverse, the virtual and physical worlds converge, creating more interactive, contextual, and immersive experiences. The ability to interact with physical objects, capture real-world data, and simulate real-world conditions enhances the authenticity and engagement within the metaverse ecosystem.

Chapter 5. Metaverse Applications

The metaverse has a wide range of applications across various industries and sectors. Here are some examples of how the metaverse can be applied:

Gaming and Entertainment: Gaming is one of the most prominent applications of the metaverse. Virtual worlds within the metaverse offer immersive gaming experiences, multiplayer interactions, and the ability to create and customize virtual avatars. Players can explore vast virtual environments, engage in quests and missions, socialize with other players, and participate in virtual events and competitions.

Social Networking and Communication: The metaverse provides a platform for social networking and communication, allowing users to connect and interact with friends, family, and like-minded individuals in virtual environments. Users can attend virtual gatherings, concerts, conferences, and engage in real-time conversations through voice chat, video calls, or text messaging. The metaverse facilitates social connections and fosters online communities.

Education and Training: The metaverse has significant potential in the field of education and training. Virtual classrooms, immersive simulations, and interactive learning experiences can be created within the metaverse. Students can engage in collaborative projects, attend virtual lectures and workshops, and explore historical or scientific environments. The metaverse offers new opportunities for distance learning, skill development, and practical training.

Virtual Commerce and Retail: The metaverse serves as a virtual marketplace, enabling virtual commerce and retail experiences. Users can browse and purchase virtual goods, clothing, accessories, and other virtual assets within the metaverse. Virtual stores and virtual fashion shows allow users to try and customize virtual products before making a purchase. Additionally, virtual real estate and land can be bought, sold, and developed within the metaverse.

Healthcare and Telemedicine: The metaverse can revolutionize healthcare by offering virtual healthcare services, telemedicine consultations, and remote patient monitoring. Virtual clinics and hospitals within the metaverse can provide medical assistance, mental health support, and health education. Virtual reality can be used for pain management, rehabilitation, and therapeutic interventions.

Architecture and Design: Architects and designers can use the metaverse to create virtual models and simulations of buildings, cities, and spaces. Virtual reality tools within the metaverse enable stakeholders to visualize and experience architectural designs before construction. The metaverse allows for collaborative design processes, real-time feedback, and immersive walkthroughs.

Virtual Workspaces and Collaboration: The metaverse offers collaborative workspaces where individuals and teams can work together remotely. Virtual offices, meeting rooms, and productivity tools facilitate remote collaboration, project management, and communication. Users can share documents, brainstorm ideas, and collaborate on virtual whiteboards, enhancing remote work capabilities.

Cultural and Artistic Experiences: The metaverse provides a platform for cultural and artistic experiences. Virtual museums, galleries, and exhibitions allow users to explore and interact with art, artifacts, and cultural heritage from around the world. Artists can showcase their work, host virtual performances, and engage with audiences in immersive and creative ways.

These are just a few examples of the diverse applications of the metaverse. As the technology and concept continue to evolve, new and innovative use cases are likely to emerge, transforming various industries and shaping the future of digital experiences.

5.1 Entertainment and Media

Entertainment and media play a significant role in the metaverse, offering immersive and interactive experiences to users. Here are some ways in which entertainment and media are incorporated into the metaverse:

Virtual Worlds and Gaming: Gaming is a major component of entertainment in the metaverse. Virtual worlds are created within the metaverse, offering players the ability to explore, interact, and engage in various gaming experiences. Players can participate in multiplayer games, engage in quests and missions, and compete with others. Virtual reality (VR) and augmented reality (AR) technologies enhance the immersion and realism of gaming experiences within the metaverse.

Virtual Events and Performances: The metaverse provides a platform for hosting and attending virtual events, concerts, performances, and conferences. Users can join in real-time or pre-recorded virtual events where they can watch live streams of performances, interact with performers, and socialize with other attendees. Virtual venues within the metaverse can replicate the atmosphere of real-world events, offering a unique and immersive entertainment experience.

Virtual Cinema and Streaming: The metaverse enables virtual cinema experiences, where users can watch movies, documentaries, and other video content within virtual theaters or screening rooms. Virtual reality headsets provide an immersive viewing environment, and users can socialize and interact with others while enjoying the content. Streaming platforms can also extend their services to the metaverse, allowing users to access their favorite shows and movies within virtual environments.

User-Generated Content and Creativity: The metaverse empowers users to create and share their own entertainment content. Users can generate virtual art, design virtual fashion, compose music, or create virtual experiences and share them with others. User-generated content platforms within the metaverse enable collaboration, creativity, and expression, fostering a vibrant community of content creators and consumers.

Advertising and Brand Engagements: Brands and advertisers can leverage the metaverse as a platform for immersive advertising and brand engagements. Virtual environments within the metaverse can incorporate branded content, virtual product placements, and interactive advertising experiences. Users can engage with branded experiences, attend virtual brand activations, and interact with virtual representations of products and services.

Sports and eSports: The metaverse offers opportunities for virtual sports and eSports experiences. Virtual stadiums and arenas can host virtual sports competitions, where users can participate in virtual versions of traditional sports or entirely new sports experiences. eSports tournaments can be held within the metaverse, attracting professional gamers and spectators from around the world.

News and Media Consumption: The metaverse can serve as a platform for news delivery and media consumption. Virtual newsrooms can provide immersive news experiences, allowing users to explore news stories, interact with journalists, and participate in virtual debates. Media organizations can create virtual content hubs within the metaverse, providing access to news articles, podcasts, videos, and other media formats.

The metaverse provides a dynamic and interactive entertainment ecosystem, where users can engage with a wide range of media and entertainment experiences. It blurs the boundaries between traditional media consumption and user participation, offering new forms of engagement, creativity, and social interaction within the digital realm.

5.2 Gaming and Esports

Gaming and eSports are integral parts of the metaverse, providing immersive and competitive experiences for players. The metaverse offers a platform where gamers can connect, compete, and engage in various gaming activities. Here's how gaming and eSports are incorporated into the metaverse:

Virtual Worlds and Environments: The metaverse consists of virtual worlds and environments specifically designed for gaming. These virtual spaces provide a backdrop for various game genres, including role-playing games (RPGs), first-person shooters (FPS), strategy games, and more. Players can explore vast virtual landscapes, interact with objects and characters, and engage in quests and missions within the metaverse.

Multiplayer Interactions: The metaverse enables multiplayer interactions, allowing players to connect and play with others from around the world. Whether it's cooperative gameplay or competitive matches, players can team up, collaborate, or compete against each other within virtual environments. The metaverse facilitates real-time interactions, voice chat, and communication features that enhance the social aspects of gaming.

Virtual Avatars and Customization: In the metaverse, players can create and customize virtual avatars that represent themselves in the gaming world. They can personalize their avatars' appearance, clothing, accessories, and abilities. Virtual currency or in-game purchases can be used to acquire new customization options, providing players with a sense of individuality and self-expression.

eSports Competitions and Tournaments: The metaverse is an ideal platform for eSports competitions and tournaments. Players can participate in organized eSports events within virtual arenas or stadiums. These events can range from small-scale tournaments to large-scale championships with professional gamers competing for prizes. Spectators can watch the matches in real-time, either within the metaverse or through live streams.

Spectator Experiences: The metaverse enhances the spectator experience for gaming and eSports. Virtual venues within the metaverse allow spectators to watch matches, tournaments, and eSports events in a virtual environment. Spectators can interact with each other, cheer for their favorite teams, and engage in virtual social interactions related to the event. Virtual reality (VR) and augmented reality (AR) technologies can further enhance the immersion and engagement of spectators.

User-Generated Content and Modding: The metaverse encourages user-generated content and modding within gaming communities. Players can create and share their own game modifications, custom levels, and virtual assets. This fosters creativity and collaboration among gamers, allowing them to contribute to the evolving gaming ecosystem within the metaverse.

Gaming Community and Social Features: The metaverse provides a platform for gamers to connect and engage with like-minded individuals. Gaming communities can form within the metaverse, where players can join guilds, clans, or social groups. These communities facilitate discussions, collaboration, and social interactions centered around gaming interests.

Cross-Platform Gaming: The metaverse enables cross-platform gaming, allowing players using different devices or platforms to interact and play together. Players on PC, console, mobile, or virtual reality platforms can connect within the metaverse, breaking down traditional barriers and expanding the gaming community.

The metaverse revolutionizes gaming and eSports by offering immersive virtual environments, enhanced multiplayer interactions, and opportunities for social engagement. It creates a dynamic and interconnected gaming ecosystem where players can compete, socialize, and explore virtual worlds together. As the metaverse continues to evolve, it is expected to further transform the gaming and eSports landscape, providing new possibilities for both players and spectators.

5.3 Healthcare and Telemedicine

Healthcare and telemedicine have significant potential within the metaverse, offering innovative ways to deliver healthcare services, facilitate remote consultations, and enhance patient experiences. Here's how healthcare and telemedicine can be integrated into the metaverse:

Virtual Clinics and Hospitals: The metaverse can host virtual clinics and hospitals where users can seek healthcare services. Patients can interact with virtual healthcare professionals, schedule appointments, and receive medical consultations within the metaverse. Virtual environments can be designed to mimic real-world healthcare settings, providing a familiar and immersive experience.

Telemedicine Consultations: Telemedicine can be seamlessly integrated into the metaverse, allowing patients to consult with healthcare providers remotely. Through virtual reality (VR) or augmented reality (AR) technologies, patients can engage in face-to-face consultations with doctors, share medical records, and receive diagnoses and treatment recommendations. The metaverse provides a convenient and accessible platform for remote healthcare services.

Remote Patient Monitoring: The metaverse can support remote patient monitoring by integrating with wearable devices and sensors. Patient health data, such as vital signs, activity levels, and medication adherence, can be collected through IoT devices and transmitted to the metaverse. Healthcare providers can monitor patients' health remotely and provide timely interventions when necessary.

Health Education and Training: The metaverse offers opportunities for health education and training. Virtual environments can be used to simulate medical scenarios, allowing healthcare professionals to practice and enhance their skills. Patients can access virtual educational resources, attend virtual health workshops, and learn about various health topics within the metaverse.

Therapeutic and Rehabilitation Applications: Virtual reality (VR) applications within the metaverse can be used for therapeutic purposes. VR environments can provide immersive experiences for pain management, anxiety reduction, and rehabilitation. Patients can engage in virtual therapy sessions, guided relaxation exercises, and interactive rehabilitation programs within the metaverse.

Health and Wellness Applications: The metaverse can support health and wellness applications, promoting healthy behaviors and lifestyle choices. Virtual environments can offer virtual fitness classes, guided meditation sessions, and personalized wellness programs. Users can track their health metrics, set goals, and receive virtual coaching within the metaverse.

Medical Research and Collaboration: The metaverse can facilitate medical research and collaboration among healthcare professionals. Virtual research labs and collaborative workspaces within the metaverse allow researchers from different locations to work together, share data, and conduct virtual experiments. This accelerates the pace of medical research and fosters collaboration in the healthcare field.

Mental Health Support: The metaverse can provide virtual environments for mental health support and therapy. Users can access virtual support groups, counseling sessions, and mental health resources within the metaverse. VR technologies can create immersive and therapeutic environments for managing mental health conditions and promoting emotional well-being.

By integrating healthcare and telemedicine into the metaverse, healthcare providers can reach a wider patient population, improve access to healthcare services, and enhance the patient experience. The metaverse offers a unique and immersive platform for healthcare delivery, allowing for more personalized, convenient, and patient-centered care.

5.4 Education and Learning

Education and learning in the metaverse have the potential to transform traditional educational models by offering immersive and interactive experiences. Here's how education and learning can be facilitated within the metaverse:

Virtual Classrooms and Learning Spaces: The metaverse can host virtual classrooms and learning spaces where students and teachers can connect and interact. Virtual environments within the metaverse can replicate the traditional classroom setting, providing a platform for lectures, discussions, and collaborative activities. Students can attend virtual classes, participate in group projects, and engage with course materials.

Immersive Simulations and Experiences: The metaverse enables immersive simulations and experiences that enhance learning outcomes. Virtual reality (VR) and augmented reality (AR) technologies within the metaverse can create realistic and interactive simulations for various subjects, such as science, history, and engineering. Students can engage in hands-on experiments, explore historical or scientific environments, and gain practical knowledge in a safe and controlled virtual space.

Collaborative Learning and Group Activities: The metaverse fosters collaborative learning by allowing students to work together on projects and assignments. Virtual group spaces within the metaverse facilitate real-time collaboration, document sharing, and interactive brainstorming sessions. Students can engage in peer-to-peer learning, exchange ideas, and develop teamwork skills, regardless of their physical locations.

Distance Learning and Accessible Education: The metaverse enables distance learning and expands access to education. Students from remote or underserved areas can access educational resources and participate in virtual classes within the metaverse. Virtual classrooms eliminate geographical barriers and provide equal learning opportunities for students worldwide. Additionally, the metaverse can accommodate diverse learning styles and needs, making education more inclusive and accessible.

Personalized Learning Experiences: The metaverse allows for personalized learning experiences tailored to individual student needs and preferences. Through data analytics and artificial intelligence (AI), the metaverse can track student progress, adapt content to their learning styles, and provide personalized recommendations. Students can learn at their own pace, receive targeted feedback, and access customized educational content within the metaverse.

Virtual Libraries and Resources: The metaverse can host virtual libraries and educational resources, providing access to a vast collection of digital books, research materials, and educational content. Students can explore virtual libraries, conduct research, and access curated resources within the metaverse. Virtual librarians or AI assistants can assist students in finding relevant information and supporting their learning journeys.

Professional Development and Lifelong Learning: The metaverse supports professional development and lifelong learning by offering virtual workshops, training programs, and certifications. Professionals can enhance their skills, learn new technologies, and stay updated on industry trends within the metaverse. Virtual networking events and career fairs within the metaverse facilitate connections between learners and professionals in various fields.

Gamified Learning and Edutainment: The metaverse can incorporate gamified learning and edutainment elements to engage students and make learning more enjoyable. Virtual reality (VR) and augmented reality (AR) technologies within the metaverse can gamify educational content, creating interactive challenges, quizzes, and educational games. This promotes active learning, motivation, and retention of knowledge.

By leveraging the metaverse for education and learning, institutions can provide immersive, engaging, and personalized learning experiences. The metaverse offers new avenues for collaboration, accessibility, and innovation in education, transforming the way knowledge is acquired and shared.

5.5 Retail and E-Commerce

Retail and e-commerce play a significant role in the metaverse, offering virtual marketplaces and immersive shopping experiences for users. Here's how retail and e-commerce are integrated into the metaverse:

Virtual Marketplaces: The metaverse provides virtual marketplaces where users can browse and purchase virtual goods, digital assets, and virtual experiences. These marketplaces can be accessed through virtual storefronts within the metaverse or through dedicated platforms that connect buyers and sellers. Users can explore a wide range of virtual products, including virtual fashion items, virtual real estate, virtual collectibles, and more.

Virtual Stores and Showrooms: Retailers can establish virtual stores and showrooms within the metaverse. These virtual spaces mimic real-world retail environments, allowing users to browse and interact with virtual products. Virtual reality (VR) and augmented reality (AR) technologies within the metaverse enhance the shopping experience by providing a realistic representation of products and allowing users to visualize them in their own virtual spaces.

Virtual Try-On and Fitting Rooms: The metaverse offers virtual try-on and fitting room experiences, enabling users to virtually try on clothing, accessories, and other fashion items. Users can create virtual avatars or upload their own images to see how different products look on them. This enhances the online shopping experience by providing a more accurate representation of the fit and style of products.

Personalization and Recommendation Engines: The metaverse leverages data analytics and artificial intelligence (AI) to personalize the shopping experience. Recommendation engines within the metaverse can suggest relevant products based on user preferences, browsing history, and behavior. Users can receive personalized product recommendations, discounts, and promotions tailored to their interests and shopping patterns.

Social Shopping and Virtual Social Interactions: The metaverse allows for social shopping experiences where users can shop together with friends or interact with other shoppers. Virtual environments within the metaverse facilitate social interactions, allowing users to chat, share recommendations, and seek advice from others. Users can also attend virtual shopping events, fashion shows, or brand activations, fostering a sense of community and social engagement.

Virtual Payments and Cryptocurrencies: The metaverse supports virtual payment systems, allowing users to make transactions within virtual marketplaces. Virtual currencies or cryptocurrencies can be used for buying and selling virtual goods and services. Blockchain technology within the metaverse ensures secure and transparent transactions, enabling trust and reliability in the virtual economy.

Brand Experiences and Advertising: Brands can create virtual brand experiences within the metaverse to engage with users. Virtual activations, events, and collaborations can be hosted within the metaverse to promote brand awareness and interact with customers. Virtual advertising and product placements can be incorporated into virtual environments, allowing brands to reach a highly engaged audience.

Virtual Customer Support: The metaverse provides opportunities for virtual customer support and assistance. Users can access virtual customer service representatives or AI-powered chatbots within virtual stores to seek product information, ask questions, and receive support. Virtual customer support can enhance the shopping experience by providing immediate assistance and resolving customer queries.

By integrating retail and e-commerce into the metaverse, businesses can tap into a new and immersive shopping environment. The metaverse offers a unique combination of social interaction, personalization, and virtual experiences, providing users with an engaging and convenient way to discover and purchase products. It expands the possibilities of online retail, creating new avenues for customer engagement and brand building.

5.6 Finance and Cryptocurrencies

Finance and cryptocurrencies play a significant role in the metaverse, providing a virtual economy and enabling secure transactions within the virtual environment. Here's how finance and cryptocurrencies are integrated into the metaverse:

Virtual Currency and Tokens: The metaverse operates on its own virtual currency or tokens that users can use for buying and selling virtual goods and services. These virtual currencies or tokens are often blockchain-based, providing security, transparency, and traceability in transactions. Users can acquire virtual currency through various means, such as purchasing or earning them through in-world activities.

Digital Asset Ownership: The metaverse allows users to own and trade digital assets, including virtual real estate, virtual fashion items, virtual collectibles, and more. Blockchain technology ensures verifiable ownership and authenticity of these digital assets. Users can buy, sell, and trade digital assets within the metaverse, creating a virtual marketplace for unique and valuable items.

Decentralized Finance (DeFi): The metaverse can incorporate decentralized finance (DeFi) applications, providing financial services such as lending, borrowing, and yield farming within the virtual economy. DeFi protocols can enable users to participate in decentralized lending and borrowing, earn interest on their virtual assets, and engage in other financial activities within the metaverse.

Virtual Banking and Payment Solutions: The metaverse can support virtual banking and payment solutions, allowing users to store their virtual currencies, manage their assets, and conduct virtual transactions. Virtual banks within the metaverse can offer services such as virtual wallets, virtual debit cards, and cross-platform payment integration, making it convenient for users to manage their financial activities within the virtual environment.

NFTs (Non-Fungible Tokens): Non-fungible tokens (NFTs) have gained significant popularity in the metaverse. NFTs represent unique digital assets or collectibles that can be bought, sold, and traded within the metaverse. These assets can include virtual artwork, virtual fashion items, virtual real estate, and more. NFTs provide provenance, scarcity, and ownership verification for digital assets, creating new opportunities for creators and collectors within the metaverse.

Virtual Investment and Trading: The metaverse can offer virtual investment and trading opportunities, allowing users to invest in virtual assets and trade virtual securities. Users can engage in virtual stock trading, virtual forex trading, and other investment activities within the metaverse. Virtual investment platforms and exchanges can facilitate these activities, providing a virtual marketplace for users to trade and speculate on virtual assets.

Virtual Crowdfunding and Initial Coin Offerings (ICOs): The metaverse can facilitate virtual crowdfunding and initial coin offerings (ICOs) for virtual projects and initiatives. Users can contribute virtual currencies to support virtual startups, virtual games, virtual worlds, and other virtual ventures within the metaverse. Virtual crowdfunding platforms and smart contracts ensure transparency and accountability in these fundraising activities.

Regulatory and Compliance Frameworks: As the metaverse evolves, there will be a need for regulatory and compliance frameworks to govern financial activities within the virtual environment. This may involve implementing virtual financial regulations, addressing anti-money laundering (AML) and know-your-customer (KYC) requirements, and ensuring the security of virtual financial transactions.

The integration of finance and cryptocurrencies into the metaverse creates a virtual economy that enables secure and transparent transactions, ownership of digital assets, and new financial opportunities. The metaverse provides a dynamic and immersive environment for users to engage in financial activities, creating a virtual financial ecosystem that complements the real-world financial systems.

Chapter 6. Societal and Cultural Implications

The metaverse has significant societal and cultural implications that can shape various aspects of human life. Here are some of the key implications:

Social Interaction and Community Building: The metaverse offers new avenues for social interaction and community building. Users can connect with people from around the world, transcending geographical boundaries. Virtual environments within the metaverse foster the formation of virtual communities based on shared interests, hobbies, and identities. This can lead to the development of new social norms, online identities, and virtual relationships.

Digital Inclusion and Accessibility: The metaverse has the potential to promote digital inclusion and accessibility. It can provide opportunities for individuals who face physical limitations or social barriers to engage in meaningful experiences. Virtual environments within the metaverse can be designed to accommodate diverse needs, making it more inclusive for people with disabilities. However, it is crucial to address the digital divide and ensure that access to the metaverse is available to all individuals.

Privacy and Security Concerns: The metaverse raises concerns about privacy and security. As users engage in virtual environments and interact with others, there is a need to protect personal information, prevent unauthorized access, and ensure data security. The collection and use of user data within the metaverse should be governed by robust privacy policies and transparent practices to build trust among users.

Virtual Identity and Self-Expression: The metaverse allows users to create virtual identities and explore different forms of self-expression. Users can design avatars, choose virtual appearances, and represent themselves in ways that may differ from their physical identities. This opens up new possibilities for personal exploration, self-representation, and identity formation within the virtual space.

Economic Opportunities and Digital Workforce: The metaverse creates new economic opportunities and a digital workforce. Users can engage in virtual commerce, virtual entrepreneurship, and virtual employment within the metaverse. This can reshape traditional job markets, blur the boundaries between work and leisure, and introduce new forms of digital labor. It is important to consider labor rights, fair compensation, and job security in the evolving metaverse economy.

Intellectual Property and Copyright: The metaverse raises challenges related to intellectual property and copyright. The creation and distribution of virtual assets, digital art, and virtual experiences within the metaverse require clear regulations and frameworks to protect the rights of creators. Issues such as plagiarism, ownership, and licensing of virtual content need to be addressed to ensure fair and ethical practices within the metaverse.

Ethical and Moral Considerations: The metaverse poses ethical and moral considerations that require careful examination. Virtual environments can replicate real-world scenarios and behaviors, including both positive and negative aspects. This raises questions about virtual ethics, appropriate conduct, and the potential impact of virtual experiences on real-world behavior. The development of ethical guidelines and responsible practices within the metaverse becomes crucial to ensure a safe and respectful virtual environment.

Cultural Exchange and Global Collaboration: The metaverse enables cultural exchange and global collaboration on an unprecedented scale. Users from different cultural backgrounds can interact, share ideas, and collaborate within virtual environments. This can promote cross-cultural understanding, creativity, and innovation. However, it also requires awareness and respect for cultural differences to avoid misunderstandings or cultural appropriation within the metaverse.

As the metaverse continues to evolve, it is essential to address these societal and cultural implications to create an inclusive, ethical, and sustainable virtual environment that enriches human experiences and enhances well-being. It calls for collaboration between stakeholders, including technology developers, policymakers, and users, to shape the metaverse in a way that aligns with societal values and respects individual rights.

6.1 Connectivity and Social Interaction

Connectivity and social interaction are fundamental aspects of the metaverse, enabling users to connect, communicate, and interact with others within virtual environments. Here are some key points regarding connectivity and social interaction in the metaverse:

Global Connectivity: The metaverse leverages the power of the internet to connect users from around the world. It provides a platform for global connectivity, allowing individuals to transcend geographical boundaries and interact with others irrespective of their physical location. Users can engage in real-time communication, collaboration, and socialization within virtual environments.

Real-time Communication: The metaverse offers various modes of real-time communication to facilitate social interaction. Users can engage in text-based chat, voice chat, or even video chat within virtual environments. These communication channels enable users to interact, share ideas, and express themselves, fostering meaningful social connections and collaboration.

Avatar-Based Interaction: In the metaverse, users typically interact with each other through avatars, representing their virtual presence. Avatars act as digital embodiments of individuals, allowing them to express their identities and engage in social interactions. Users can customize their avatars' appearance, behavior, and characteristics, enhancing self-expression and enabling diverse forms of interaction.

Social Networking and Friendships: The metaverse incorporates social networking features that enable users to build connections and form friendships. Users can create profiles, add friends, and maintain social networks within the virtual environment. Social interactions within the metaverse can extend beyond virtual environments, fostering relationships and connections that transcend the boundaries of the virtual world.

Shared Virtual Spaces: The metaverse provides shared virtual spaces where users can gather, collaborate, and socialize. These spaces can include virtual worlds, virtual events, virtual clubs, and other community-oriented areas. Users can engage in shared activities, attend virtual gatherings, and participate in virtual experiences together, creating a sense of belonging and community.

Social Presence and Emotion Expression: The metaverse allows users to express their social presence and emotions within virtual environments. Through avatars, users can convey body language, gestures, and facial expressions, enabling a more nuanced and immersive form of social interaction. Users can express their emotions, share experiences, and establish emotional connections with others in the metaverse.

Virtual Events and Activities: The metaverse hosts virtual events and activities that promote social interaction and engagement. Users can participate in virtual conferences, concerts, exhibitions, parties, and other gatherings within the virtual environment. These events provide opportunities for networking, entertainment, and shared experiences, enhancing social interaction in the metaverse.

Cross-Platform Connectivity: The metaverse aims to provide cross-platform connectivity, allowing users to connect and interact across different devices and platforms. Users can access the metaverse through virtual reality (VR) headsets, augmented reality (AR) devices, personal computers, smartphones, and other connected devices. This cross-platform connectivity enhances the accessibility and reach of social interactions within the metaverse.

Connectivity and social interaction in the metaverse form the foundation for building communities, fostering collaboration, and promoting a sense of presence and engagement. The metaverse strives to create immersive and interactive virtual environments that enable meaningful connections and social experiences, transforming the way individuals interact and socialize in the digital realm.

6.2 Creativity and Collaboration

Creativity and collaboration are at the core of the metaverse, empowering users to explore their imagination, work together, and co-create within virtual environments. Here are some key aspects of creativity and collaboration in the metaverse:

User-Generated Content: The metaverse encourages users to create and share their content. Users can contribute to the development of virtual worlds, objects, avatars, animations, and other digital assets within the metaverse. This user-generated content fuels creativity and enables individuals to express their ideas, skills, and artistic abilities.

Virtual Design and Creation Tools: The metaverse provides tools and platforms that facilitate virtual design and creation. Users can utilize intuitive and accessible tools to build virtual environments, 3D models, interactive experiences, and more. These tools empower users with varying levels of technical expertise to bring their creative visions to life within the metaverse.

Collaborative Creation: The metaverse allows for collaborative creation, enabling multiple users to work together on shared projects. Users can collaborate in real-time, regardless of their physical locations, to build virtual worlds, develop virtual products, and co-create immersive experiences. Collaboration tools within the metaverse facilitate real-time communication, simultaneous editing, and joint decision-making.

Virtual Art and Expression: The metaverse serves as a canvas for virtual art and expression. Artists can create virtual paintings, sculptures, installations, and immersive experiences that go beyond the limitations of the physical world. The metaverse provides a platform for showcasing and sharing virtual art, enabling artists to reach global audiences and explore new forms of creative expression.

Cross-Disciplinary Collaboration: The metaverse brings together individuals from diverse backgrounds and disciplines. It fosters cross-disciplinary collaboration, where artists, designers, programmers, storytellers, musicians, and other creative professionals can collaborate and merge their skills to create unique and immersive experiences within the metaverse. This cross-pollination of ideas and expertise fuels innovation and pushes the boundaries of what is possible.

Virtual Events and Performances: The metaverse hosts virtual events, concerts, performances, and exhibitions that leverage technology to create immersive and interactive experiences. These events allow artists, musicians, performers, and other creative professionals to showcase their talents, engage with audiences, and experiment with new forms of creative expression. Virtual events within the metaverse provide opportunities for collaboration, audience participation, and global reach.

Remix Culture and Mashups: The metaverse fosters a remix culture, where users can take existing virtual assets, modify them, and create something new. Users can remix virtual environments, objects, and media to create unique combinations and mashups. This culture of remixing and mashups encourages experimentation, innovation, and the continuous evolution of virtual content within the metaverse.

Crowdsourcing and Collective Intelligence: The metaverse enables crowdsourcing and collective intelligence. Users can leverage the collective knowledge, skills, and creativity of the community to solve problems, generate ideas, and co-create projects. Virtual communities within the metaverse can collaborate on shared goals, pooling resources and expertise to achieve collective outcomes.

Creativity and collaboration within the metaverse empower individuals and communities to explore, experiment, and co-create in a digital realm. The metaverse provides a fertile ground for innovation, artistic expression, and collaborative endeavors, fostering a dynamic and vibrant ecosystem of creativity and collaboration.

6.3 Privacy and Security Concerns

Privacy and security concerns are significant considerations in the development and adoption of the metaverse. As users engage in virtual environments and interact with others, there are several key privacy and security considerations that need to be addressed:

Data Privacy: The metaverse involves the collection, storage, and processing of user data. It is crucial to establish robust privacy policies and practices to protect user privacy. Clear guidelines should be in place regarding the collection, use, and sharing of personal information within the metaverse. Users should have control over their data and be able to make informed decisions about how their information is used.

Identity Protection: In the metaverse, users often create virtual identities represented by avatars. It is essential to ensure that users' virtual identities are protected and not easily linked to their real-world identities. Safeguards should be implemented to prevent unauthorized access to personal information and protect against identity theft or impersonation.

Online Harassment and Bullying: Virtual environments within the metaverse can be prone to online harassment, bullying, and other forms of negative behavior. Measures should be in place to address and mitigate such issues. Reporting mechanisms, content moderation, and community guidelines can help create a safe and respectful environment for users.

Cybersecurity: The metaverse requires robust cybersecurity measures to protect against hacking, data breaches, and other cyber threats. Virtual environments and platforms should implement strong authentication mechanisms, encryption protocols, and regular security audits. Security updates and patches should be promptly deployed to address vulnerabilities.

Virtual Asset Theft and Fraud: The metaverse involves the creation, ownership, and trade of virtual assets. It is important to protect users against virtual asset theft and fraud. Secure systems should be implemented to ensure the ownership and transfer of virtual assets, including digital currencies and unique digital items. Smart contracts and blockchain technology can be utilized to establish transparent and secure transactions.

Informed Consent and Permissions: Users should have control over their participation and sharing of information within the metaverse. Clear consent mechanisms should be implemented, ensuring that users are informed about the collection and use of their data. Users should have the ability to grant or revoke permissions for data sharing and adjust their privacy settings according to their preferences.

Cross-Platform Data Sharing: The metaverse spans across various platforms and devices, requiring data sharing and interoperability. It is essential to establish secure protocols for cross-platform data sharing to protect user privacy and prevent unauthorized access to personal information as users move between different virtual environments and services.

Ethical Use of Data and AI: As data is collected and analyzed within the metaverse, ethical considerations should guide its use. Artificial intelligence (AI) algorithms that process user data should adhere to principles of fairness, transparency, and accountability. Bias and discrimination should be actively addressed, and users should have clear visibility into how their data is being used to personalize their experiences.

Addressing these privacy and security concerns in the metaverse requires collaboration between platform developers, policymakers, and users. A combination of technical measures, user education, and transparent policies can help create a metaverse that respects user privacy, fosters a secure environment, and builds trust among its participants.

6.4 Digital Addiction and Well-being

As the metaverse becomes more immersive and engaging, there are concerns about the potential for digital addiction and its impact on well-being. Here are some considerations regarding digital addiction and well-being in the metaverse:

Excessive Engagement: The metaverse offers a wide range of experiences and activities that can captivate users for extended periods. Spending excessive time in virtual environments may lead to neglecting real-world responsibilities, relationships, and self-care activities, potentially impacting overall well-being.

Escapism and Detachment: The immersive nature of the metaverse may provide an escape from real-world challenges or emotions. Individuals may be tempted to spend increasing amounts of time in the metaverse to avoid facing real-life difficulties. This detachment from reality can have negative consequences on mental health, social interactions, and personal growth.

Physical Health Implications: Extensive use of the metaverse often involves sedentary behavior, leading to a lack of physical activity and associated health issues. Prolonged periods of sitting or wearing virtual reality (VR) headsets can lead to discomfort, eye strain, and other physical ailments. It is important to maintain a balance between virtual and physical activities to promote overall well-being.

Social Isolation: While the metaverse offers opportunities for social interaction, there is a risk of substituting real-world social connections with virtual ones. Excessive reliance on virtual interactions may lead to social isolation, diminishing the quality and depth of real-life relationships. It is crucial to maintain a healthy balance between virtual and face-to-face interactions to support social well-being.

Emotional Well-being: Engaging in the metaverse can evoke a range of emotions, both positive and negative. Excessive exposure to virtual environments and experiences may impact emotional well-being, causing addiction-like behavior, mood swings, or emotional dependency on virtual interactions. It is important to prioritize emotional self-care, maintaining awareness of one's feelings and seeking support when needed.

Mindfulness and Self-Reflection: The metaverse can be a stimulating and distracting environment, making it challenging to engage in mindful practices or self-reflection. Taking regular breaks, setting boundaries, and consciously allocating time for self-reflection can help individuals maintain a healthy relationship with the metaverse and support overall well-being.

Parental Guidance and Education: Children and adolescents are particularly vulnerable to the potential negative effects of excessive metaverse engagement. Parental guidance, education, and setting appropriate usage limits can help ensure their well-being and promote a healthy relationship with technology.

Responsible Design and Regulation: Platform developers and policymakers have a role to play in promoting responsible design and regulation of the metaverse. This includes implementing features that encourage healthy usage, providing tools for self-monitoring and managing screen time, and adopting ethical guidelines to protect user well-being.

Balancing the benefits of the metaverse with potential risks is crucial for promoting well-being. Encouraging responsible use, maintaining awareness of personal boundaries, nurturing real-world connections, and fostering a healthy relationship with technology are essential for individuals to thrive both in the metaverse and the physical world.

6.5 Ethical Considerations and Inclusivity

Ethical considerations and inclusivity play a crucial role in shaping the metaverse and ensuring it is a positive and equitable space for all users. Here are some key aspects of ethical considerations and inclusivity in the metaverse:

Accessibility: The metaverse should strive to be accessible to individuals with diverse abilities. This includes providing options for different interaction modalities, such as text-based communication for individuals with hearing impairments, and ensuring virtual environments are designed with considerations for individuals with visual impairments or mobility challenges. Accessibility features should be implemented to enable equal participation and engagement.

Diversity and Inclusion: The metaverse should reflect and celebrate the diversity of its user base. Efforts should be made to ensure the representation and inclusion of individuals from different backgrounds, cultures, genders, and identities. This can be achieved through customizable avatars, inclusive virtual environments, and policies that discourage discrimination, hate speech, or harassment. Promoting diversity and fostering inclusive communities within the metaverse creates a welcoming and enriching experience for all users.

Privacy and Consent: Respecting user privacy and obtaining informed consent are essential ethical considerations in the metaverse. Clear guidelines and policies should be in place to protect user data, ensuring that personal information is collected and used transparently and with explicit user consent. Users should have control over their data and the ability to manage their privacy settings and permissions.

Content Moderation: Content moderation is critical to maintain a safe and inclusive metaverse. Implementing robust moderation policies and practices helps prevent the spread of harmful or offensive content, harassment, or discriminatory behavior. Moderation should be performed transparently and consistently, striking a balance between freedom of expression and the protection of user well-being.

Algorithmic Bias and Fairness: Algorithms and AI systems used within the metaverse should be designed to minimize bias and ensure fairness. Bias in recommendation systems, content filtering, and avatar customization should be actively addressed to prevent discriminatory outcomes. Ethical guidelines and diversity considerations should inform the design and training of AI models to promote fairness and inclusivity.

Digital Well-being: The metaverse should prioritize the well-being of its users and encourage healthy usage patterns. This includes implementing features that promote breaks, limit excessive screen time, and provide tools for self-monitoring and managing virtual engagement. Educating users about digital well-being practices and supporting mental health resources within the metaverse can contribute to a healthier user experience.

Transparent Governance and Regulation: Transparent governance and regulation frameworks are necessary to ensure accountability and uphold ethical standards within the metaverse. Stakeholder involvement, open dialogue, and collaboration between platform developers, policymakers, user communities, and advocacy groups can help shape policies and guidelines that prioritize ethical considerations and inclusivity.

Continuous Evaluation and Improvement: Ethical considerations and inclusivity should be an ongoing focus within the metaverse. Regular evaluation, user feedback, and collaboration with relevant stakeholders can help identify areas for improvement and ensure ethical practices are continually evolving to meet the changing needs and expectations of the user community.

By actively addressing ethical considerations and promoting inclusivity, the metaverse can become a space that fosters positive interactions, celebrates diversity, and empowers users to express themselves authentically while ensuring the protection of user rights and well-being.

Chapter 7. Building the Metaverse

Building the metaverse is a complex and multidimensional task that requires collaboration from various stakeholders, including technology companies, developers, content creators, policymakers, and user communities. Here are some key considerations and steps involved in building the metaverse:

Technological Infrastructure: The metaverse requires a robust technological infrastructure to support the creation, hosting, and delivery of virtual environments, content, and experiences. This includes scalable cloud computing resources, high-speed internet connectivity, edge computing capabilities, and efficient data storage and processing systems.

Interoperability and Standards: Interoperability is crucial for the metaverse to enable seamless interactions between different platforms, virtual worlds, and devices. The development of open standards and protocols allows for the exchange of data, assets, and services across various metaverse components. Collaboration among stakeholders is necessary to establish interoperability standards that foster a cohesive and interconnected metaverse ecosystem.

Content Creation Tools: User-generated content is a fundamental aspect of the metaverse. Building intuitive and accessible content creation tools empowers users to contribute their creativity and shape the virtual environments. These tools should cater to a wide range of users, from professional developers to casual creators, enabling them to design, build, and customize virtual objects, worlds, and experiences.

Virtual Reality (VR) and Augmented Reality (AR) Technologies: VR and AR technologies are central to the metaverse experience, providing immersive and interactive elements. Continued advancements in VR and AR hardware, software, and user interfaces are necessary to enhance the realism and engagement of the metaverse. This includes improvements in display resolution, tracking systems, input devices, and haptic feedback technologies.

Data Management and Privacy: The metaverse generates vast amounts of user data, including personal information, preferences, and behavior patterns. Robust data management practices and privacy protections are essential to establish user trust and comply with data protection regulations. Clear policies should be in place to outline how data is collected, used, and secured, with transparent consent mechanisms and user controls.

Artificial Intelligence (AI) and Machine Learning (ML): AI and ML technologies can enhance the metaverse by enabling intelligent interactions, content personalization, and dynamic experiences. AI algorithms can assist with content curation, recommendation systems, natural language processing, and computer vision tasks within the metaverse. Responsible AI practices should be implemented to ensure fairness, transparency, and ethical use of AI in the metaverse.

Community Engagement and Governance: Building the metaverse requires active engagement with user communities and stakeholders. Inclusive governance models that involve diverse perspectives can help shape policies, guidelines, and standards for the metaverse. Community feedback and collaboration can drive innovation, address concerns, and ensure the metaverse evolves in a way that benefits its users.

Iterative Development and User Feedback: The development of the metaverse is an iterative process that requires continuous improvement based on user feedback and market dynamics. Regular user testing, surveys, and feedback loops help identify areas for enhancement, usability issues, and emerging user needs. Agile development methodologies can facilitate rapid iteration and responsiveness to evolving user expectations.

Partnerships and Collaboration: Building the metaverse is a collaborative endeavor that requires partnerships among technology companies, content creators, academic institutions, and policymakers. Collaboration can drive innovation, knowledge sharing, and the exchange of best practices. Public-private partnerships can facilitate research, funding, and regulatory frameworks that support the development and responsible growth of the metaverse.

Building the metaverse is an ongoing journey, with new technologies, trends, and user expectations continually shaping its evolution. It requires a holistic approach that considers technological advancements, ethical considerations, inclusivity, and user-centric design to create a vibrant, interconnected, and immersive digital realm.

7.1 Technical Considerations and Challenges

Building the metaverse involves several technical considerations and challenges. Here are some key aspects to consider:

Scalability and Performance: The metaverse aims to support a massive number of users concurrently interacting in virtual environments. Ensuring the scalability and performance of the underlying infrastructure, including servers, networks, and databases, is crucial to handle the high demand and maintain a seamless user experience.

Latency and Responsiveness: Real-time interactions are a fundamental aspect of the metaverse. Minimizing latency and ensuring responsive communication between users, platforms, and virtual environments is essential to create a sense of presence and enable fluid interactions. This requires optimizing network connectivity, minimizing data transmission delays, and employing technologies like edge computing to reduce round-trip times.

Interoperability and Standards: The metaverse consists of diverse platforms, virtual worlds, and devices. Establishing interoperability standards, protocols, and APIs that enable seamless communication and content exchange between different components is necessary for a cohesive and connected metaverse experience. Standardizing formats, data structures, and interaction models can foster interoperability among various metaverse entities.

Data Management and Storage: The metaverse generates massive amounts of data, including user profiles, virtual assets, and real-time interactions. Efficient data management and storage systems are required to handle the volume, variety, and velocity of data generated within the metaverse. Implementing scalable and distributed databases, content delivery networks (CDNs), and data caching mechanisms can help manage and retrieve data effectively.

Security and Privacy: As the metaverse becomes more interconnected, ensuring the security and privacy of user data, transactions, and interactions becomes paramount. Robust authentication mechanisms, encryption protocols, and access control mechanisms should be implemented to protect user information and prevent unauthorized access or data breaches. Privacy regulations and policies should be followed to handle personal data responsibly.

Content Creation and Management: The metaverse relies on user-generated content and experiences. Providing intuitive and powerful content creation tools, asset management systems, and content moderation mechanisms is essential to enable users to contribute to the metaverse easily. Implementing content filtering, moderation processes, and user reporting mechanisms helps maintain a safe and appropriate metaverse environment.

Artificial Intelligence (AI) and Machine Learning (ML): AI and ML technologies play a significant role in the metaverse, enhancing user experiences, personalization, and content recommendation. Developing and deploying AI models that can process and analyze vast amounts of data in real-time is essential. Challenges include training AI models on diverse and dynamic metaverse data, addressing bias in AI algorithms, and ensuring transparency and interpretability of AI-driven processes.

User Experience Design: Creating an immersive and engaging user experience in the metaverse requires thoughtful design and consideration of usability principles. Designing intuitive user interfaces, seamless navigation, and responsive interactions is crucial. Balancing realism, performance, and user comfort in virtual reality (VR) and augmented reality (AR) experiences is also a challenge that requires optimizing hardware capabilities and reducing motion sickness.

Cross-Platform Compatibility: The metaverse encompasses various platforms, including desktops, mobile devices, VR headsets, and AR glasses. Ensuring cross-platform compatibility and providing consistent experiences across different devices and form factors can be challenging. Developing applications and interfaces that adapt to the capabilities and constraints of each platform is necessary for a seamless metaverse experience.

Energy Consumption: The metaverse's growth and increasing demand for computing resources can have environmental implications. Minimizing energy consumption, optimizing server infrastructure, and promoting sustainable practices are essential to reduce the environmental impact of the metaverse.

Addressing these technical considerations and challenges requires a collaborative effort among technology companies, developers, researchers, and other stakeholders. Continuous innovation, research, and improvement are necessary to build a robust and sustainable metaverse that delivers compelling experiences while ensuring scalability, security, privacy, and usability.

7.2 Content Creation and Curation

Content creation and curation are vital aspects of the metaverse, as they contribute to the richness and diversity of experiences within virtual environments. Here are key considerations for content creation and curation in the metaverse:

User-Generated Content (UGC): The metaverse encourages user-generated content, empowering individuals to create and contribute their virtual assets, worlds, and experiences. UGC allows for a diverse range of creativity and personalization, fostering a dynamic and engaging metaverse ecosystem.

Content Creation Tools: Providing intuitive and accessible content creation tools is essential to enable users with varying levels of technical expertise to contribute to the metaverse. These tools should support a wide range of media formats, such as 3D models, textures, animations, audio, and video, and offer features for object manipulation, scene composition, and scripting.

Intellectual Property Rights: Addressing intellectual property rights is crucial in the metaverse. Establishing clear guidelines, licensing frameworks, and mechanisms to protect creators' rights and prevent unauthorized use or plagiarism of content helps ensure a fair and ethical metaverse environment. Smart contracts and blockchain-based solutions can facilitate copyright protection and transparent attribution of ownership.

Content Moderation: Implementing content moderation mechanisms is essential to maintain a safe and inclusive metaverse. Content moderation processes should be in place to detect and handle inappropriate, offensive, or harmful content. Combining automated algorithms with human moderation teams can help ensure a balance between user freedom and responsible content curation.

Content Discovery and Recommendation: With the abundance of content in the metaverse, effective content discovery and recommendation systems are necessary to help users navigate and find relevant experiences. AI-driven algorithms can analyze user preferences, behavior, and social connections to provide personalized recommendations, facilitating content exploration and serendipitous discovery.

Curated Experiences and Events: Curating special experiences and events within the metaverse adds excitement and engagement. This can include virtual concerts, art exhibitions, gaming tournaments, educational workshops, and social gatherings. Curated experiences help drive community interaction, showcase talented creators, and create unique moments that attract and retain users.

Quality Assurance and Feedback: Ensuring quality standards for metaverse content is important to maintain a positive user experience. Establishing quality assurance processes, feedback loops, and rating systems enables users to provide feedback on content and experiences, helping creators improve their work and fostering a culture of continuous improvement.

Collaboration and Co-Creation: The metaverse encourages collaboration and co-creation among users. Enabling shared creative spaces, collaborative tools, and real-time collaboration features allows users to work together on projects, create jointly, and build vibrant virtual communities. Collaborative experiences promote engagement, knowledge sharing, and collective innovation.

Monetization and Incentives: Providing avenues for content creators to monetize their work is essential for sustaining the metaverse ecosystem. Various models, such as virtual item sales, subscriptions, advertising, or crowdfunding, can be explored. Implementing fair revenue-sharing mechanisms and creating incentives for creators can encourage high-quality content generation and foster a vibrant creator community.

Ethical and Inclusive Content: Encouraging ethical content creation and promoting inclusivity is important in the metaverse. Platforms should establish guidelines and policies that discourage hate speech, discrimination, or harmful content. Promoting diverse representation, cultural sensitivity, and respecting the rights and identities of all users contribute to a welcoming and inclusive metaverse environment.

Content creation and curation in the metaverse are ongoing processes that require collaboration between platform providers, content creators, and user communities. Striking a balance between user-generated content and curated experiences, while addressing ethical considerations, helps create a vibrant and engaging metaverse for all participants.

7.3 User Experience and Interface Design

User experience (UX) and interface design play a crucial role in the metaverse, as they shape how users interact with virtual environments, navigate through content, and engage with others. Here are key considerations for user experience and interface design in the metaverse:

Immersive and Intuitive Interactions: Designing interfaces that provide immersive and intuitive interactions is essential in the metaverse. The goal is to create interfaces that feel natural and allow users to navigate, interact with objects, and communicate with others in a seamless and intuitive manner. This may involve using gestures, voice commands, haptic feedback, and spatial computing to enhance the sense of presence and immersion.

Seamless Onboarding and Orientation: Ensuring a smooth onboarding process for new users is important to reduce barriers to entry. Providing clear instructions, interactive tutorials, and guidance within the virtual environment can help users understand the metaverse's features, controls, and navigation, allowing them to quickly get acquainted with the interface and start exploring.

Responsive and Adaptive Design: The metaverse encompasses various devices, including desktop computers, mobile devices, VR headsets, and AR glasses. Designing interfaces that adapt to different screen sizes, resolutions, and input methods is crucial to provide a consistent and optimized user experience across platforms. Responsive design principles can be applied to ensure usability and readability across a range of devices.

Contextual Feedback and Guidance: Providing contextual feedback and guidance is essential to help users understand the outcomes of their actions and make informed decisions. Visual cues, tooltips, and contextual notifications can be used to provide real-time feedback and guide users through various interactions and activities within the metaverse.

Efficient Information Architecture: Organizing and presenting information in a clear and structured manner is crucial in the metaverse. Well-designed information architecture allows users to easily locate content, navigate through menus and options, and find relevant information. Using hierarchical structures, search functionalities, and filtering options can help users efficiently explore and access the vast amount of content available.

Social Interaction and Communication: Facilitating social interaction and communication is a key aspect of the metaverse. Designing interfaces that enable seamless communication channels, such as voice chat, text chat, and video conferencing, helps users connect and collaborate with others. Emphasizing social presence cues, such as avatars and real-time presence indicators, can enhance the sense of connectedness and community.

Personalization and Customization: Allowing users to personalize and customize their virtual experiences fosters a sense of ownership and engagement. Providing options to customize avatars, virtual spaces, preferences, and interface layouts allows users to tailor their metaverse experience to their preferences and identity.

Accessibility and Inclusivity: Designing for accessibility and inclusivity is essential in the metaverse. Considering diverse user needs, such as visual impairments, hearing impairments, and motor disabilities, helps ensure that the metaverse is accessible to all users. Implementing features like alternative text for images, closed captioning, and support for assistive technologies promotes inclusivity.

Consistency and Visual Hierarchy: Maintaining consistency in design elements and visual hierarchy helps users navigate and understand the interface more easily. Consistent placement of navigation menus, icons, and controls, along with clear visual cues, enhances usability and reduces cognitive load. Applying visual hierarchy principles, such as using size, color, and contrast, helps draw attention to important elements and content.

User Testing and Iterative Design: Conducting user testing and gathering feedback throughout the design process is crucial to refine the user experience. Iterative design cycles allow for continuous improvement based on user insights and needs. Incorporating user feedback, conducting usability tests, and observing user behavior helps identify pain points and optimize the interface design for better user engagement and satisfaction.

Designing the user experience and interface in the metaverse requires a deep understanding of user needs, technology capabilities, and the unique context of virtual environments. Continual iteration, user research, and a user-centered design approach are key to creating immersive, intuitive, and engaging experiences in the metaverse.

7.4 Interoperability and Standards

Interoperability and standards are crucial considerations in the development of the metaverse. They enable seamless communication, collaboration, and content exchange between different platforms, virtual worlds, and devices. Here's an overview of interoperability and standards in the metaverse:

Interoperability: Interoperability refers to the ability of different systems and components to work together and exchange information effectively. In the metaverse, interoperability allows users to seamlessly navigate between different virtual environments, communicate with users on different platforms, and transfer assets and data across platforms.

Cross-Platform Communication: Interoperability standards enable users on one platform to interact and communicate with users on another platform. This can involve protocols for voice chat, text chat, video conferencing, and other forms of communication. Standards like WebRTC (Web Real-Time Communication) and the Open Metaverse Interoperability Group (OMG) work towards enabling cross-platform communication.

Asset and Content Exchange: Interoperability standards facilitate the transfer and exchange of virtual assets and content between different platforms and virtual worlds. These standards define file formats, encoding schemes, and metadata structures that ensure compatibility and seamless transfer of assets such as 3D models, textures, animations, and audio files.

Identity and Authentication: Interoperability standards for identity and authentication enable users to maintain a consistent identity across different metaverse platforms. These standards provide mechanisms for secure authentication, single sign-on, and identity verification, ensuring that users can access their accounts and maintain their digital presence seamlessly across platforms.

Data and APIs: Standardized data formats and application programming interfaces (APIs) enable platforms and applications in the metaverse to exchange data and interact with each other. Open APIs and data standards allow developers to create applications and services that can integrate with multiple platforms, facilitating cross-platform functionality and data sharing.

Decentralized Standards and Protocols: Blockchain technology plays a role in facilitating interoperability in the metaverse through decentralized standards and protocols. Blockchain-based platforms, such as Ethereum, are exploring standards like ERC-721 (Non-Fungible Token) and ERC-1155 (Multi-Token Standard) for interoperability of digital assets across different metaverse platforms.

Open Standards and Consortia: Several industry initiatives and consortia are working towards establishing open standards for the metaverse. These organizations bring together technology companies, developers, and other stakeholders to collaborate on defining protocols, formats, and guidelines that promote interoperability. Examples include the Decentralized Identity Foundation (DIF), Khronos Group, and the Immersive Digital Experiences Alliance (IDEA).

Metadata and Search Standards: Metadata standards play a role in facilitating content discovery and search in the metaverse. Metadata describes various attributes of virtual assets, such as titles, descriptions, tags, and categorizations, allowing users to find relevant content. Standards like the Dublin Core Metadata Initiative and Schema.org provide frameworks for describing and organizing metadata in a consistent manner.

Establishing interoperability and standards in the metaverse requires collaboration and consensus among industry stakeholders. It involves defining common protocols, formats, and practices that enable seamless communication, content exchange, and user experiences across different platforms and virtual worlds. By promoting interoperability, the metaverse can foster a connected and unified digital environment that transcends individual platforms and enables broader collaboration and innovation.

7.5 Scalability and Infrastructure

Scalability and infrastructure are critical factors in the development and success of the metaverse. As the metaverse grows in terms of users, content, and interactions, it requires robust and scalable infrastructure to support the increasing demands. Here are some considerations for scalability and infrastructure in the metaverse:

Network Infrastructure: The metaverse relies on a robust network infrastructure to facilitate real -time communication, data transfer, and interactions between users and virtual environments. High-speed internet connectivity, low latency, and reliable network connections are essential to ensure a seamless and immersive metaverse experience.

Server and Cloud Infrastructure: The metaverse requires powerful server and cloud infrastructure to handle the computational requirements of rendering complex virtual environments, managing user interactions, and supporting large-scale concurrency. Distributed server architectures, edge computing, and cloud-based solutions help distribute the processing load and ensure scalability and performance.

Content Delivery Networks (CDNs): CDNs play a crucial role in delivering content, such as 3D assets, textures, and multimedia, to users in the metaverse. CDNs optimize content distribution by caching data closer to end-users, reducing latency and improving overall performance. CDNs help alleviate the strain on servers and ensure efficient content delivery, particularly for globally distributed user bases.

Scalable Database Systems: As the metaverse generates vast amounts of data, scalable and efficient database systems are necessary to handle user profiles, asset metadata, transaction records, and other persistent data. Distributed and scalable database architectures, such as NoSQL databases and sharding techniques, help handle the growing data volumes and ensure fast and reliable data access.

Computational Power and Graphics Processing: Rendering realistic virtual environments and supporting advanced graphics require significant computational power. High-performance GPUs (Graphics Processing Units) and specialized hardware accelerators play a vital role in providing the processing capabilities needed for immersive experiences in the metaverse. Advancements in hardware technology, such as ray tracing and real-time rendering, enhance visual quality and realism.

Data Storage and Archiving: The metaverse generates a vast amount of data, including user-generated content, virtual world data, and transactional information. Scalable and resilient data storage solutions, including distributed file systems, object storage, and archival systems, ensure efficient data management, data persistence, and data retrieval in the metaverse.

API and Integration Infrastructure: The metaverse relies on APIs and integration infrastructure to enable seamless interactions between different platforms, services, and applications. Well-defined APIs, standards, and integration frameworks facilitate the exchange of data, assets, and functionalities, enabling interoperability and the creation of innovative metaverse experiences.

Load Balancing and Resource Management: As the metaverse experiences spikes in user activity and concurrent interactions, load balancing techniques and resource management strategies become crucial. Load balancers distribute incoming traffic across multiple servers to prevent overloading and ensure optimal performance. Resource management systems monitor resource utilization and allocate computational resources efficiently, ensuring a smooth user experience even during peak usage.

Security and Privacy Infrastructure: Scalability and infrastructure considerations must also address security and privacy concerns in the metaverse. Robust security measures, including encryption, access controls, and authentication mechanisms, are necessary to protect user data, virtual assets, and transactions. Privacy-enhancing technologies and compliance with data protection regulations help ensure user privacy in the metaverse.

Continuous Monitoring and Optimization: Scalability and infrastructure requirements in the metaverse are dynamic and evolve over time. Continuous monitoring, performance testing, and optimization processes are necessary to identify bottlenecks, optimize resource utilization, and proactively address scalability challenges. This iterative approach ensures that the infrastructure keeps pace with the growing demands of the metaverse.

Building a scalable and robust infrastructure for the metaverse is an ongoing process that requires collaboration between technology providers, platform developers, and infrastructure providers. As the metaverse expands, advancements in networking, computing, and storage technologies will continue to drive its scalability and pave the way for innovative virtual experiences.

7.6 Security and Privacy

Security and privacy are paramount considerations in the metaverse due to the potential risks associated with virtual interactions, data exchange, and user identities. Here are some key aspects of security and privacy in the metaverse:

User Authentication and Identity Protection: Robust authentication mechanisms are essential to ensure that users are who they claim to be and to prevent unauthorized access to virtual environments and user accounts. Multi-factor authentication, biometric authentication, and decentralized identity systems can enhance security in the metaverse. Protecting user identities and personal information from theft or misuse is crucial to maintain user trust.

Data Encryption and Secure Communication: Encryption techniques, such as Transport Layer Security (TLS), are vital to secure data transmission within the metaverse. End-to-end encryption can safeguard sensitive user information and communications, preventing unauthorized access and eavesdropping. Secure communication protocols are essential for protecting user privacy and ensuring the confidentiality of interactions.

Access Controls and Permissions: Implementing access controls and permission systems helps protect virtual environments and digital assets from unauthorized modifications or misuse. Role-based access control (RBAC) mechanisms can ensure that users have appropriate permissions to perform certain actions within the metaverse. Granular access controls can be applied to different aspects, such as virtual spaces, objects, and user-generated content.

Virtual Asset Security: As virtual assets hold value in the metaverse, protecting them from theft, fraud, or unauthorized duplication is critical. Blockchain technology, through the use of non-fungible tokens (NFTs) and smart contracts, can provide transparent ownership records and secure transactions for virtual assets. Secure storage and transfer mechanisms for virtual assets, combined with robust ownership verification, can mitigate security risks.

User Privacy and Data Protection: Safeguarding user privacy and personal data is essential in the metaverse. Platforms and services must comply with relevant data protection regulations and implement privacy-enhancing measures, such as data anonymization, consent management, and data minimization. Transparency in data handling practices and clear privacy policies can help users make informed decisions about their personal information.

Protection Against Malicious Activities: Measures should be in place to prevent and mitigate malicious activities, including hacking, phishing, and identity theft. Security protocols, regular vulnerability assessments, and proactive monitoring can help detect and prevent security breaches. Reporting mechanisms for suspicious activities and efficient response systems are crucial to maintain the overall security of the metaverse.

User Empowerment and Control: Giving users control over their personal data and privacy settings is important. Providing clear options for privacy preferences, data sharing, and consent management empowers users to make choices aligned with their preferences. Transparent data handling practices and user-friendly privacy controls can enhance user trust and confidence in the metaverse.

Education and Awareness: Promoting security and privacy awareness among users is essential to mitigate risks in the metaverse. Education initiatives can help users understand potential threats, best practices for secure interactions, and strategies to protect their personal information. Platforms and service providers can play a role in educating users about security measures and privacy safeguards.

Collaboration and Industry Standards: Collaboration among metaverse stakeholders, including platform developers, technology providers, and regulatory bodies, is crucial to establish industry standards and best practices for security and privacy. Sharing security insights, threat intelligence, and adopting common security frameworks can enhance the overall security posture of the metaverse.

Ethical Considerations: Ensuring ethical practices in the metaverse involves respecting user rights, fostering inclusivity, and avoiding discrimination. Ethical considerations should be integrated into security and privacy measures to promote a safe and inclusive metaverse environment.

Security and privacy in the metaverse require a multi-layered approach, combining technological solutions, user awareness, and industry collaboration. By prioritizing security and privacy, the metaverse can foster a trusted and secure digital space for users to explore, interact, and create.

Chapter 8. Metaverse Economics and Business Models

The metaverse introduces new possibilities for economic activities and business models, transforming how value is created, exchanged, and monetized in virtual environments. Here are some key aspects of metaverse economics and business models:

Virtual Assets and Digital Economies: The metaverse enables the creation and trade of virtual assets, including virtual currencies, digital goods, and virtual real estate. Virtual assets hold value within the metaverse ecosystem, and users can buy, sell, and trade them. Digital economies emerge, driven by supply and demand dynamics, where users can monetize their creations and engage in virtual commerce.

Virtual Currency and Tokens: Virtual currencies, often specific to individual metaverse platforms, serve as mediums of exchange within the virtual economies. Cryptocurrencies and blockchain-based tokens are also used in some metaverse environments, providing secure and decentralized transactions. Virtual currencies and tokens can be earned through activities, purchased with real-world currencies, or acquired through gameplay.

Digital Goods and Services: The metaverse offers a marketplace for digital goods and services, such as virtual clothing, accessories, avatars, virtual real estate, and virtual experiences. Users can create and sell their own digital assets or engage in virtual commerce with others. Digital goods can be sold through platforms or peer-to-peer transactions, generating revenue for creators and platform operators.

Advertising and Brand Sponsorship: Brands and advertisers can leverage the metaverse as a new channel for advertising and brand sponsorships. Virtual spaces, events, and experiences can be sponsored, allowing brands to reach a highly engaged and targeted audience. In-world product placements, virtual billboards, and branded virtual items are some examples of advertising opportunities within the metaverse.

Subscription and Membership Models: Some metaverse platforms offer subscription-based or membership models, granting users access to exclusive features, content, or services. Subscriptions can provide a recurring revenue stream for platform operators and offer enhanced benefits and privileges to subscribers.

Virtual Real Estate and Land Ownership: Virtual real estate represents digital spaces within the metaverse that users can own, develop, and monetize. Users can purchase and sell virtual land, create virtual buildings and structures, and generate revenue through virtual businesses and events hosted on their properties. Virtual real estate can be leased, rented, or sold, creating economic opportunities within the metaverse.

Virtual Events and Experiences: The metaverse enables the hosting of virtual events, conferences, concerts, and exhibitions. Organizers can monetize these events through ticket sales, sponsorship deals, virtual merchandise, and virtual experiences. Virtual events provide opportunities for content creators, performers, and event organizers to reach a global audience and generate revenue.

Platform Fees and Revenue Sharing: Metaverse platforms often charge fees for transactions, sales, or services provided within the virtual ecosystem. Platform operators may take a percentage of transactions or sales made by users on their platforms. Additionally, revenue-sharing models can be employed, where creators receive a portion of the revenue generated from their virtual assets or activities.

Cross-Platform Integration and Metaverse Economy: Interoperability between metaverse platforms allows for the seamless transfer of assets and value between different virtual environments. Cross-platform integration enables a unified metaverse economy, where users can engage in commerce, social interactions, and experiences across multiple platforms, expanding the scope of economic activities.

Blockchain and Decentralized Finance (DeFi): Blockchain technology and decentralized finance (DeFi) concepts are being explored within the metaverse to enable secure and transparent transactions, ownership verification, and decentralized governance. Smart contracts and blockchain-based platforms can facilitate peer-to-peer transactions, decentralized marketplaces, and innovative economic models within the metaverse.

The economics and business models in the metaverse are still evolving, with new opportunities and challenges emerging as the concept continues to develop. The dynamic nature of the metaverse provides a fertile ground for experimentation and innovation in economic systems, reshaping the way value is generated and exchanged in virtual spaces.

8.1 Digital Assets and Virtual Economies

Digital assets and virtual economies play a central role in the metaverse, creating new opportunities for value creation, exchange, and economic activities. Here are some key aspects of digital assets and virtual economies in the metaverse:

Virtual Currencies: Virtual currencies serve as the medium of exchange within the metaverse. They enable users to buy, sell, and trade digital goods and services. Virtual currencies can be earned through various activities within the metaverse, such as gameplay, content creation, or virtual commerce. Examples of virtual currencies include Robux in Roblox, V-Bucks in Fortnite, and Linden Dollars in Second Life.

Digital Goods: Digital goods refer to virtual items, assets, or commodities that hold value within the metaverse. They can include virtual clothing, accessories, avatars, weapons, skins, and other in-game items. Digital goods can be created by users or offered by game developers and content creators. Users can acquire digital goods through purchases, trades, or in-game achievements.

Virtual Real Estate: Virtual real estate represents virtual land or properties within the metaverse. Users can buy, sell, and develop virtual land, creating virtual spaces for various purposes. Virtual real estate can range from private homes and businesses to virtual event venues or social gathering places. Users can monetize their virtual real estate through rental income, virtual businesses, or hosting events.

User-Created Content: User-generated content (UGC) plays a significant role in the metaverse. Users can create and sell their own digital assets, including 3D models, textures, animations, scripts, and more. UGC platforms and marketplaces allow users to monetize their creations, earning revenue through sales or royalties. UGC fosters a vibrant creative community within the metaverse.

Trading and Marketplace Platforms: Metaverse platforms provide virtual marketplaces where users can buy, sell, and trade digital assets. These platforms facilitate peer-to-peer transactions and provide tools for asset discovery, pricing, and secure exchanges. Popular virtual marketplace platforms include OpenSea, Decentraland Marketplace, and the Roblox marketplace.

NFTs (Non-Fungible Tokens): Non-fungible tokens have gained prominence in the metaverse as a way to represent unique, indivisible digital assets. NFTs provide verifiable ownership and provenance for digital items, including artwork, collectibles, virtual real estate, and more. NFTs are often based on blockchain technology, enabling secure and transparent ownership records.

Virtual Economies and Inflation: Virtual economies within the metaverse are subject to supply and demand dynamics, creating value fluctuations and market trends. Some virtual economies may experience inflation, where the supply of digital goods and virtual currencies exceeds demand, leading to price increases and devaluation. Economic policies, such as adjusting item drop rates or virtual currency issuance, can influence virtual economies.

Monetization Models: Various monetization models are employed in the metaverse, including direct purchases, subscriptions, microtransactions, and freemium models. Developers and content creators generate revenue by selling digital goods, offering premium content or features, or providing exclusive experiences. Users can choose to invest in the metaverse through purchases, supporting content creators, or participating in virtual commerce.

Real-World Exchange and Value Conversion: Some digital assets in the metaverse have real-world value, and users may seek to convert them into traditional currencies. Exchange platforms facilitate the conversion of virtual currencies or digital assets into fiat currencies or cryptocurrencies. Third-party marketplaces also allow users to trade virtual assets for real-world goods or services.

Economic Governance and Regulations: As virtual economies grow, issues such as taxation, fraud, and scams may arise. Governments and regulatory bodies are starting to explore frameworks for managing virtual economies and ensuring consumer protection. Platforms and virtual communities may also implement governance models and policies to maintain fair economic practices.

Digital assets and virtual economies create opportunities for individuals, content creators, businesses, and platform operators to participate in the metaverse economy. As the metaverse continues to evolve, the value and impact of digital assets within virtual economies are likely to expand, leading to new economic possibilities and challenges.

8.2 Monetization Strategies

Monetization strategies in the metaverse revolve around generating revenue from virtual experiences, digital goods, and services. Here are some common monetization strategies employed in the metaverse:

Virtual Item Sales: One of the primary monetization strategies is selling virtual items, such as virtual clothing, accessories, avatars, or in-game items. Users can purchase these items using virtual currencies or real-world currencies. Developers and content creators can offer a wide range of virtual items with different price points to cater to various user preferences.

Virtual Real Estate Sales and Rentals: Virtual real estate can be monetized through sales or rentals. Users can purchase virtual land or properties within the metaverse and develop them for various purposes. They can then rent out their virtual properties to other users, host events, or create virtual businesses to generate income.

Subscriptions and Memberships: Offering subscription-based access or membership tiers can be an effective monetization strategy. Users can subscribe to premium features, exclusive content, or enhanced experiences. Subscription models provide recurring revenue and incentivize users to engage more deeply with the metaverse platform or community.

Virtual Events and Experiences: Hosting virtual events and experiences can be monetized through ticket sales or entry fees. These events can include virtual concerts, conferences, exhibitions, or immersive experiences. By offering unique and engaging virtual experiences, organizers can generate revenue while providing valuable entertainment or educational opportunities.

Advertising and Brand Partnerships: Advertising and brand partnerships can be a significant revenue stream in the metaverse. Brands can sponsor virtual spaces, events, or digital content, reaching a highly engaged audience. In-world product placements, virtual billboards, or branded virtual items can also generate advertising revenue.

Royalties from User-Created Content: Platforms that allow users to create and sell their own digital content can implement a revenue-sharing model. Content creators earn royalties or a percentage of the sales when their digital creations are purchased by other users. This incentivizes creativity and fosters a vibrant creator community within the metaverse.

Platform Fees and Commissions: Metaverse platforms often charge fees or commissions on transactions made within their ecosystem. For example, they may take a percentage of virtual item sales, virtual real estate transactions, or in-world commerce. Platform fees help sustain and support the development and maintenance of the metaverse platform.

Partnerships and Collaborations: Collaborating with other brands, influencers, or content creators can lead to monetization opportunities. Partnerships can involve co-branded virtual items, cross-promotion, or revenue-sharing arrangements. By leveraging existing audiences and resources, partners can expand their reach and generate shared revenue.

Sponsored Challenges and Competitions: Organizing sponsored challenges or competitions within the metaverse can attract user participation and generate revenue. Sponsors provide prizes or rewards for winners, while benefiting from brand exposure and engagement. This monetization strategy enhances user engagement and fosters a competitive environment.

Virtual Services and Consultations: Offering virtual services or consultations can be monetized in the metaverse. This includes services like virtual coaching, consulting, design, or virtual world development. Users can hire experts or professionals to provide personalized services or guidance within the metaverse.

It's important for metaverse platforms and developers to strike a balance between monetization and user experience. Providing value to users through high-quality experiences, unique content, and fair pricing is crucial for sustainable monetization in the metaverse.

8.3 Startups and Entrepreneurship in the Metaverse

Startups and entrepreneurship in the metaverse are thriving as the concept continues to gain momentum. The metaverse provides a fertile ground for innovative ideas, new business models, and entrepreneurial ventures. Here are some key aspects of startups and entrepreneurship in the metaverse:

Virtual Businesses and Services: Entrepreneurs can establish virtual businesses and offer a wide range of services within the metaverse. This can include virtual real estate development, content creation, event organization, virtual fashion design, virtual marketing agencies, virtual world consulting, and more. Virtual businesses can cater to the needs of metaverse users, providing them with valuable products or services.

User-Created Content Platforms: Platforms that enable users to create and monetize their digital content in the metaverse have gained popularity. These platforms allow entrepreneurs to build businesses around supporting and empowering content creators. By providing tools, resources, and marketplaces for user-generated content, entrepreneurs can generate revenue through transaction fees, subscriptions, or advertising.

Metaverse Infrastructure and Tools: Entrepreneurs can focus on building infrastructure, technologies, and tools that support the metaverse ecosystem. This can include developing virtual reality (VR) and augmented reality (AR) hardware, software platforms, content creation tools, virtual marketplaces, blockchain-based solutions, virtual event platforms, and more. Entrepreneurs in this space contribute to the foundation and growth of the metaverse.

Virtual Events and Experiences: Startups can specialize in organizing and delivering virtual events and experiences within the metaverse. They can offer services such as virtual event production, virtual concert management, virtual conferences, virtual trade shows, and immersive virtual experiences. Entrepreneurs can leverage the unique capabilities of the metaverse to create engaging and interactive virtual events.

Virtual Reality (VR) and Augmented Reality (AR) Experiences: With the increasing popularity of VR and AR technologies, startups can focus on developing immersive experiences that blend the physical and virtual worlds. They can create VR games, AR applications, virtual museums, training simulations, virtual tours, and more. Entrepreneurs in this space are at the forefront of merging virtual and real-world experiences.

Social Platforms and Communities: Startups can create social platforms or virtual communities within the metaverse, catering to specific niches or interests. These platforms can facilitate social interactions, networking, and collaboration among metaverse users. Entrepreneurs can monetize these platforms through advertising, subscriptions, or virtual item sales.

Virtual Commerce and E-Commerce Solutions: Entrepreneurs can develop innovative solutions for virtual commerce within the metaverse. This includes creating virtual marketplaces, payment gateways, secure trading platforms, virtual storefronts, and integration with real-world e-commerce systems. By enabling seamless and secure virtual commerce, startups contribute to the growth of the metaverse economy.

Virtual Education and Learning: Startups can focus on virtual education and learning platforms within the metaverse. They can create virtual classrooms, training simulations, language learning apps, and educational content for users to enhance their skills and knowledge in immersive virtual environments. Entrepreneurs can monetize these platforms through subscriptions, course fees, or partnerships with educational institutions.

Virtual Health and Wellness: The metaverse can also be leveraged for virtual health and wellness startups. Entrepreneurs can develop virtual fitness applications, mental health support platforms, virtual therapy sessions, and wellness-focused virtual experiences. Startups in this space aim to enhance well-being and provide accessible virtual health services.

Blockchain and Cryptocurrency Solutions: Entrepreneurs can explore the intersection of blockchain technology and the metaverse. They can develop blockchain-based solutions for virtual asset ownership, secure transactions, decentralized marketplaces, and virtual currency systems. Startups can contribute to building a transparent and secure metaverse ecosystem.

Startups and entrepreneurs in the metaverse face both opportunities and challenges. It is crucial for them to understand the unique dynamics of the metaverse, create innovative and engaging experiences, and foster strong communities to succeed in this evolving landscape.

8.4 Job Opportunities and Future Workforce

The emergence of the metaverse creates a wide range of job opportunities and shapes the future workforce in several ways. Here are some key aspects of job opportunities and the future workforce in the metaverse:

Virtual World Designers and Developers: With the growth of the metaverse, there is an increasing demand for professionals who can design and develop virtual worlds and experiences. These professionals are skilled in areas such as 3D modeling, virtual environment design, programming, and user experience design.

Virtual Economists and Data Analysts: As virtual economies flourish within the metaverse, the need for virtual economists and data analysts arises. These professionals analyze user behavior, virtual market trends, and economic patterns to optimize virtual economies, ensure balance, and make data-driven decisions.

Content Creators and Digital Artists: The metaverse thrives on user-generated content and digital art. Content creators and digital artists play a vital role in producing virtual assets, including 3D models, textures, animations, music, and visual effects. Their skills contribute to the richness and diversity of the metaverse.

Virtual Event Organizers and Moderators: Virtual events, conferences, and social gatherings are becoming increasingly common in the metaverse. Virtual event organizers and moderators are responsible for planning, coordinating, and hosting these events. They manage logistics, engage participants, and ensure smooth operations within the virtual environment.

Virtual Educators and Trainers: With the integration of education and learning in the metaverse, virtual educators and trainers are in demand. These professionals design and deliver virtual courses, training programs, and educational experiences. They leverage the immersive and interactive nature of the metaverse to enhance learning outcomes.

Virtual Architects and Designers: The metaverse offers opportunities for virtual architecture and design professionals. They are involved in designing virtual buildings, spaces, and environments within the metaverse. Virtual architects and designers bring their expertise to create visually appealing and functional virtual structures.

Virtual Fashion Designers and Stylists: Fashion plays a significant role in the metaverse, with users customizing their virtual avatars and dressing them in virtual clothing and accessories. Virtual fashion designers and stylists create virtual fashion lines, design avatars' appearances, and stay updated with the latest fashion trends in the metaverse.

AI and ML Specialists: Artificial intelligence (AI) and machine learning (ML) technologies are integral to the metaverse. AI and ML specialists contribute to the development of intelligent virtual characters, chatbots, recommendation systems, and personalized user experiences within the metaverse.

Blockchain Experts: Blockchain technology is being integrated into the metaverse for asset ownership, secure transactions, and digital identity management. Blockchain experts are sought after to design and implement blockchain-based solutions within the metaverse ecosystem.

Community Managers and Social Moderators: Building and nurturing communities is crucial for the success of the metaverse. Community managers and social moderators engage with users, manage online communities, resolve conflicts, and maintain a positive and inclusive virtual environment.

As the metaverse continues to evolve, new job roles and opportunities will emerge. The future workforce in the metaverse will require a combination of technical skills, creativity, adaptability, and a deep understanding of virtual environments and user behavior. Continuous learning and a willingness to embrace new technologies will be essential for professionals entering the metaverse job market.

Chapter 9. Legal and Regulatory Landscape

The legal and regulatory landscape of the metaverse is still evolving as the concept continues to develop. Given the complexity and wide-ranging nature of the metaverse, there are several legal and regulatory considerations that need to be addressed. Here are some key aspects of the legal and regulatory landscape of the metaverse:

Intellectual Property Rights: Protecting intellectual property (IP) within the metaverse is a significant concern. This includes copyrights, trademarks, and patents related to virtual content, virtual assets, and virtual worlds. Clear guidelines and mechanisms are needed to address IP infringement, licensing, and ownership disputes in the metaverse.

Privacy and Data Protection: The collection, storage, and use of user data within the metaverse raise privacy concerns. Data protection regulations and policies need to be established to safeguard user information. Users should have control over their personal data and be informed about how it is being used within the metaverse.

Digital Identity and Authentication: The metaverse relies on digital identities for user interactions and transactions. Ensuring secure digital identity management and authentication is crucial. Legal frameworks should address issues such as identity theft, fraud prevention, and the verification of virtual identities.

Virtual Asset Ownership and Trading: Clear rules and regulations are needed to define and protect virtual asset ownership within the metaverse. This includes virtual currencies, virtual real estate, virtual items, and other virtual assets. Establishing legal frameworks for virtual asset trading, taxation, and dispute resolution is essential.

Consumer Protection: Consumer protection laws play a role in regulating transactions and ensuring fair practices within the metaverse. This includes transparent pricing, accurate product descriptions, refund policies, and protection against fraudulent activities. Regulations should address issues such as virtual item scams and misleading advertising.

Anti-Money Laundering (AML) and Know Your Customer (KYC): As virtual currencies and virtual asset trading gain prominence in the metaverse, it becomes important to prevent money laundering and ensure compliance with KYC regulations. Establishing AML and KYC procedures within the metaverse can help mitigate illicit activities.

Platform Liability and Content Moderation: Metaverse platforms need to establish policies and guidelines regarding user-generated content, hate speech, harassment, and illegal activities. Platforms may be held liable for the content and actions of their users, necessitating clear guidelines and mechanisms for content moderation and user behavior enforcement.

Jurisdictional Challenges: The metaverse transcends physical borders, creating challenges in determining jurisdiction and applicable laws. Resolving jurisdictional issues and harmonizing legal frameworks across different regions is a complex task. International collaboration and agreements may be necessary to address jurisdictional challenges.

Competition and Antitrust: As the metaverse evolves, competition and antitrust considerations may arise. Ensuring fair competition, preventing monopolistic practices, and promoting innovation within the metaverse are important aspects of the legal and regulatory landscape.

Ethical and Social Considerations: The metaverse raises ethical and social considerations that may require legal and regulatory attention. This includes issues related to virtual violence, addiction, virtual property rights, virtual relationships, and the impact on real-world societies. Establishing guidelines and regulations that promote ethical behavior and protect vulnerable individuals is crucial.

It's important to note that the legal and regulatory landscape of the metaverse is still developing and varies across jurisdictions. Governments, policymakers, and industry stakeholders need to collaborate to address these considerations and strike a balance between fostering innovation and protecting user rights within the metaverse.

9.1 Intellectual Property and Copyright

Intellectual Property (IP) and copyright in the metaverse are crucial for protecting the rights of creators and fostering innovation. Here's a closer look at their implications in the metaverse:

Virtual Content: In the metaverse, creators produce a wide range of virtual content, including virtual art, virtual music, virtual literature, and virtual designs. Copyright protects these creations, giving creators exclusive rights to control the reproduction, distribution, and public display of their works.

Virtual Assets: Virtual assets, such as virtual goods, virtual clothing, virtual accessories, and virtual property, are also subject to intellectual property and copyright protection. Creators of virtual assets can claim copyright over their original designs, preventing others from reproducing or using them without permission.

Virtual Worlds: Virtual worlds within the metaverse, comprising landscapes, buildings, and interactive elements, may qualify for copyright protection. The unique architecture and design of virtual worlds can be copyrighted, preventing unauthorized replication in other metaverse environments.

User-Generated Content: The metaverse encourages user-generated content, where users create and contribute their virtual creations. It's important to consider ownership and licensing rights in such scenarios. Platforms may require users to grant specific permissions or licenses for the use of their content within the metaverse.

Licensing and Permissions: Within the metaverse, licensing and permissions play a crucial role in the use of copyrighted works. Creators can license their works to others, granting specific rights for use, distribution, and monetization. Licensing agreements define the terms and conditions for using copyrighted works in the metaverse.

Fair Use and Transformative Works: Fair use provisions allow for limited use of copyrighted works without permission, primarily for purposes such as criticism, commentary, news reporting, teaching, and research. In the metaverse, fair use may apply to transformative works that take existing content and create something new and different.

Enforcement and Digital Rights Management: Protecting intellectual property in the metaverse requires effective enforcement mechanisms and digital rights management (DRM) tools. Platforms may implement measures to prevent unauthorized copying, distribution, or alteration of copyrighted works within their virtual environments.

International Considerations: The metaverse operates on a global scale, raising international considerations for intellectual property and copyright. Intellectual property laws and copyright regulations may differ across jurisdictions, making it important to navigate legal requirements and protection mechanisms accordingly.

Creators in the metaverse should be aware of their rights and take steps to protect their intellectual property. Additionally, platforms and metaverse operators should establish clear policies and mechanisms for addressing copyright infringement, respecting intellectual property rights, and fostering a creative and collaborative environment.

9.2 Data Protection and Privacy Laws

Data protection and privacy laws play a vital role in the metaverse to ensure the privacy and security of user information. Here are some key considerations regarding data protection and privacy laws in the metaverse:

General Data Protection Regulation (GDPR): The GDPR, implemented in the European Union (EU), sets the standards for data protection and privacy. It applies to organizations that process personal data of EU residents, regardless of their location. Metaverse platforms operating in the EU or processing EU residents' personal data must comply with the GDPR's requirements, including obtaining user consent, providing transparency in data processing, and implementing appropriate security measures.

California Consumer Privacy Act (CCPA) and Similar Regulations: The CCPA, and other similar regulations like the California Privacy Rights Act (CPRA), provide data protection rights to California residents. These laws require businesses that collect personal data of California residents to disclose their data collection practices, allow users to opt-out of data sharing, and ensure the security of personal information. Platforms serving California residents must comply with these regulations.

Data Minimization and Purpose Limitation: Metaverse platforms should adhere to principles of data minimization and purpose limitation. This means collecting and retaining only necessary user data and using it for specific purposes disclosed to users. Data should not be used or retained beyond what is required.

User Consent and Control: Obtaining user consent is crucial for data processing in the metaverse. Platforms should provide clear information about the types of data collected, the purposes of processing, and user rights. Users should have control over their data, including the ability to access, rectify, delete, or restrict its processing.

Security Measures: Metaverse platforms need to implement appropriate security measures to protect user data from unauthorized access, loss, or disclosure. This includes encryption, access controls, regular data backups, and vulnerability assessments. Platforms should also have incident response plans in place to address data breaches or security incidents.

Cross-Border Data Transfers: Transferring personal data across borders may be subject to restrictions under data protection laws. In some jurisdictions, data can only be transferred to countries with an adequate level of data protection. Adequacy agreements, such as the EU-US Privacy Shield or standard contractual clauses, can be used to facilitate lawful data transfers.

Children's Privacy: The metaverse often attracts younger users, and specific privacy protections for children may apply. Laws like the Children's Online Privacy Protection Act (COPPA) in the United States require parental consent for collecting personal information from children under a certain age. Platforms should implement age verification mechanisms and parental consent processes when engaging with younger users.

Privacy Policies and Transparency: Metaverse platforms should have clear and easily accessible privacy policies that outline their data collection, use, and disclosure practices. Transparency is key to building user trust and ensuring compliance with privacy laws.

It's important for metaverse operators to stay up-to-date with relevant data protection and privacy laws in the jurisdictions they operate in. Compliance with these laws not only protects user privacy but also fosters a trustworthy and safe metaverse environment.

9.3 Governance and Regulation Challenges

Governance and regulation in the metaverse pose significant challenges due to its decentralized and global nature. Here are some key challenges associated with governance and regulation in the metaverse:

Jurisdictional Complexity: The metaverse transcends traditional jurisdictional boundaries, making it difficult to determine which laws and regulations apply. With users and platforms operating from various countries, harmonizing regulations and resolving conflicts between different legal systems becomes complex.

Lack of Consistent Standards: The metaverse lacks consistent technical and regulatory standards across different platforms and environments. This hinders interoperability and creates challenges for establishing uniform governance and regulation frameworks.

Platform Liability and Accountability: Determining platform liability and accountability for user-generated content and activities is a significant challenge. Platforms may be held responsible for illegal or harmful content shared by users, leading to complex legal and regulatory considerations.

Content Moderation and Censorship: Ensuring appropriate content moderation and addressing concerns related to censorship is a contentious issue. Balancing freedom of expression with the need to prevent harmful or illegal content poses challenges in defining and implementing content moderation policies.

Intellectual Property Rights: Protecting intellectual property rights within the metaverse is complex, as digital assets and virtual content can be easily replicated and shared. Defining ownership, licensing, and enforcement mechanisms for virtual assets and copyrighted works requires innovative approaches.

Security and Privacy: The metaverse poses security and privacy risks due to the collection and storage of user data, potential breaches, and unauthorized access. Balancing security measures with user privacy rights and establishing robust mechanisms to address cybersecurity threats is crucial.

User Protection and Consumer Rights: The metaverse needs regulations to protect users and ensure consumer rights. This includes transparent pricing, fair competition, dispute resolution mechanisms, and protection against fraud and scams within virtual transactions.

Decentralization and Governance Models: The metaverse operates on decentralized principles, with various stakeholders contributing to its development and operation. Determining governance models that accommodate decentralized decision-making while addressing regulatory requirements is a challenge.

International Collaboration and Harmonization: Given the global nature of the metaverse, international collaboration and harmonization of regulations become necessary. Cooperation between governments, industry stakeholders, and international organizations is essential to develop consistent frameworks and address governance challenges.

Ethical Considerations: The metaverse raises ethical considerations, such as virtual violence, addiction, and the impact on real-world societies. Establishing ethical guidelines and norms that promote inclusivity, fairness, and the well-being of users within the metaverse presents governance challenges.

Addressing these governance and regulation challenges requires a collaborative and iterative approach involving policymakers, industry players, legal experts, and user communities. It involves striking a balance between fostering innovation and ensuring user protection, privacy, and ethical practices within the evolving metaverse ecosystem.

10. International Collaboration and StandardsThe Future of the Metaverse

International collaboration and the development of standards are critical for the future of the metaverse. Here's why:

Interoperability and Seamless Experience: The metaverse consists of diverse platforms, technologies, and virtual environments. International collaboration can help establish interoperability standards that enable seamless communication, data sharing, and cross-platform interactions. Standards can ensure that users can navigate between different metaverse environments effortlessly, enhancing the overall user experience.

Consistent Regulation and Governance: As the metaverse transcends national borders, consistent international regulations and governance frameworks are necessary. Collaboration among countries can help harmonize legal and regulatory frameworks, addressing challenges related to jurisdiction, privacy, security, intellectual property, and consumer protection. Consistent standards can provide clarity for users, creators, and businesses operating in the metaverse.

Technical Standards and Infrastructure: Developing technical standards is crucial for the metaverse's growth and scalability. These standards can cover areas such as data formats, virtual asset representation, communication protocols, security measures, and user interface design. International collaboration can drive the development and adoption of these standards, enabling seamless integration and innovation across the metaverse ecosystem.

Trust and User Protection: International collaboration can foster trust among users and ensure their protection in the metaverse. Collaborative efforts can lead to the establishment of trust frameworks, identity management standards, data protection guidelines, and mechanisms for resolving disputes. These initiatives can enhance user confidence, encouraging broader adoption of the metaverse.

Economic Growth and Innovation: International collaboration and standards development can fuel economic growth and innovation within the metaverse. By establishing a level playing field and reducing barriers to entry, collaboration can spur entrepreneurship, investment, and job creation. Consistent standards can facilitate the development of new applications, technologies, and business models, driving the metaverse's expansion.

Social and Cultural Inclusivity: International collaboration can help ensure that the metaverse is inclusive and respects diverse cultural and societal norms. By involving stakeholders from different countries and backgrounds, standards can be shaped to promote fairness, accessibility, and cultural sensitivity. This fosters a metaverse that caters to a global audience, embracing a wide range of perspectives and experiences.

Ethical Considerations and Responsible Development: International collaboration enables the incorporation of ethical considerations into the development of the metaverse. By bringing together experts and stakeholders from various regions, discussions on topics such as digital rights, AI ethics, data ethics, and user well-being can take place. Collaborative efforts can drive the adoption of responsible practices and guidelines within the metaverse ecosystem.

International collaboration and the development of standards in the metaverse require the involvement of governments, industry players, standards organizations, academia, and user communities. Open dialogues, cooperative initiatives, and ongoing collaboration can shape the future of the metaverse, ensuring its growth, sustainability, and positive impact on society.

10.1 Emerging Trends and Technologies

The metaverse is an evolving concept that continuously incorporates emerging trends and technologies. Here are some of the prominent trends and technologies shaping the future of the metaverse:

Virtual Reality (VR) and Augmented Reality (AR): VR and AR technologies provide immersive experiences in the metaverse, blurring the line between the physical and virtual worlds. These technologies enable users to interact with virtual environments and objects, enhancing the sense of presence and immersion.

Extended Reality (XR): XR is an umbrella term that encompasses VR, AR, and mixed reality (MR). XR technologies combine real and virtual environments to create highly interactive and immersive experiences. XR allows users to engage with virtual content in a more natural and intuitive manner.

Spatial Computing: Spatial computing technologies enable the metaverse to understand and interact with physical space. These technologies use computer vision, sensor fusion, and spatial mapping to create dynamic representations of the physical environment, allowing virtual objects to interact with real-world objects and surfaces.

Haptic Feedback: Haptic feedback technologies provide tactile sensations to users in the metaverse. Through the use of wearable devices, users can experience physical sensations such as touch, pressure, and vibration, enhancing the realism and interactivity of virtual experiences.

Artificial Intelligence (AI) and Machine Learning (ML): AI and ML play a significant role in the metaverse by enhancing realism, personalization, and interactivity. AI-powered algorithms can generate realistic virtual environments, enable natural language processing for voice interactions, and provide intelligent virtual assistants within the metaverse.

Blockchain and Cryptocurrencies: Blockchain technology and cryptocurrencies have the potential to revolutionize the metaverse's economy and ownership systems. Blockchain provides decentralized and secure transactional infrastructure, enabling secure virtual asset ownership, transparent transactions, and decentralized governance models.

Edge Computing: Edge computing brings computational resources closer to the edge of the network, reducing latency and enabling faster processing of data in the metaverse. Edge computing can enhance the responsiveness and real-time interactions within virtual environments, improving the overall user experience.

Internet of Things (IoT) and Sensor Networks: IoT devices and sensor networks can bridge the physical and virtual worlds in the metaverse. These devices can capture real-time data from the physical environment, enabling virtual representations of real-world objects and enabling real-time interactions and data exchange.

5G and High-Speed Connectivity: The advent of 5G networks and high-speed connectivity provides the necessary infrastructure for seamless and real-time communication within the metaverse. These technologies support low-latency interactions, high-quality video streaming, and faster data transfer, enhancing the metaverse's capabilities.

Social VR and Collaborative Tools: Social VR platforms and collaborative tools facilitate social interactions and collaboration within the metaverse. These tools enable users to connect, communicate, and collaborate with others in virtual environments, fostering social engagement and shared experiences.

These emerging trends and technologies are continually advancing and evolving, shaping the future of the metaverse and expanding its possibilities. As technology continues to progress, the metaverse will become even more immersive, interconnected, and integrated with our daily lives.

10.2 Predictions and Speculations

Predictions and speculations about the metaverse are subject to uncertainty and the rapidly evolving nature of technology. However, here are some potential developments and speculations regarding the future of the metaverse:

Enhanced Immersive Experiences: The metaverse is expected to offer increasingly immersive experiences, leveraging technologies such as VR, AR, haptic feedback, and spatial computing. Users may be able to fully immerse themselves in highly realistic and interactive virtual environments, blurring the boundaries between the physical and virtual worlds.

Seamless Cross-Platform Interactions: Interoperability and seamless cross-platform interactions will likely become a key focus in the metaverse. Users may have the ability to transition seamlessly between different metaverse environments, bringing their virtual identities, assets, and social connections with them across various platforms and experiences.

Digital Economy and Virtual Asset Ownership: The metaverse is likely to witness the growth of a robust digital economy, where virtual assets hold significant value. Virtual currencies and blockchain technology may facilitate secure ownership, trading, and monetization of virtual assets, leading to new economic models and business opportunities.

AI-Powered Personalization: Artificial intelligence (AI) and machine learning (ML) algorithms may play a crucial role in personalizing the metaverse experience. AI could analyze user behavior, preferences, and context to dynamically generate tailored content, recommendations, and interactions within the virtual environment.

Virtual Social Networks and Communities: The metaverse is expected to foster the growth of virtual social networks and communities. Users may engage in social activities, connect with friends, participate in events, and build virtual communities based on shared interests, hobbies, or professional affiliations.

Real-Time Collaboration and Remote Work: The metaverse could transform remote work and collaboration by providing immersive and collaborative virtual workspaces. Teams dispersed across different locations could come together in the metaverse to collaborate on projects, conduct meetings, and share resources, offering new possibilities for remote work and telecommuting.

Integration with IoT and Physical Environments: The metaverse may increasingly integrate with the Internet of Things (IoT) and sensor networks, creating a deeper connection between the virtual and physical worlds. Virtual objects and environments could interact with real-world devices, enabling new applications in areas such as smart cities, healthcare, and industrial automation.

Evolution of Metaverse Governance: Governance models and regulations within the metaverse will likely evolve to address challenges related to privacy, security, content moderation, intellectual property rights, and user protection. International collaboration may play a vital role in establishing standards and frameworks for responsible governance of the metaverse.

Impact on Industries and Entertainment: The metaverse has the potential to revolutionize various industries, including gaming, entertainment, education, healthcare, retail, and more. It may reshape how we consume media, learn, socialize, shop, and access services, offering new opportunities for businesses and transforming the way we experience entertainment and media.

It's important to note that these predictions and speculations are based on current trends and technological advancements, but the actual future of the metaverse may unfold differently. The metaverse is a complex and dynamic concept, and its development will be influenced by a wide range of factors, including technological advancements, societal adoption, regulatory considerations, and user demands.

10.3 Social and Cultural Evolution

The metaverse has the potential to bring about significant social and cultural evolution. Here are some key aspects of its potential impact:

Global Connectivity and Cross-Cultural Interactions: The metaverse can connect people from different parts of the world, transcending geographical boundaries. It has the power to facilitate cross-cultural interactions and foster understanding and empathy among diverse communities. People can engage in virtual environments where cultural norms and perspectives can be shared, celebrated, and understood.

Democratization of Expression and Creativity: The metaverse provides a platform for individuals to express themselves creatively, irrespective of their background or resources. It can democratize access to tools, resources, and platforms for content creation, enabling a diverse range of voices to be heard. This can lead to the emergence of new art forms, virtual worlds, and cultural expressions.

New Social Dynamics and Communities: The metaverse can give rise to new social dynamics and communities. People can form virtual communities based on shared interests, identities, or causes, fostering a sense of belonging and connection. These communities can transcend physical limitations, bringing together individuals who may have otherwise struggled to find like-minded individuals in their immediate surroundings.

Redefining Social Norms and Identities: The metaverse offers individuals the opportunity to experiment with and redefine their social identities. People can explore different aspects of their identity, present themselves in virtual spaces differently, and challenge societal norms and expectations. This can contribute to the evolution of social norms and a greater acceptance of diverse identities and expressions.

Cultural Preservation and Heritage: The metaverse can play a role in preserving cultural heritage and traditions. Virtual environments can recreate historical sites, artifacts, and cultural practices, allowing for their preservation and accessibility to a global audience. It can also facilitate the sharing of indigenous knowledge and cultural practices, fostering cultural exchange and appreciation.

New Modes of Education and Learning: The metaverse has the potential to transform education and learning by offering immersive and interactive experiences. Virtual classrooms, educational simulations, and collaborative learning environments can enhance access to education, facilitate global knowledge sharing, and provide personalized learning experiences.

Ethical Considerations and Digital Citizenship: As the metaverse evolves, ethical considerations and digital citizenship will become increasingly important. Individuals and societies will need to navigate issues such as privacy, security, digital rights, online etiquette, and responsible use of virtual spaces. The cultural evolution of the metaverse will require ongoing discussions, collaborations, and frameworks to ensure ethical and inclusive practices.

It's important to note that the social and cultural evolution of the metaverse will be shaped by various factors, including societal values, regulatory frameworks, technological advancements, and user behaviors. While the metaverse offers opportunities for positive social and cultural change, it also poses challenges that need to be addressed collectively to create an inclusive, diverse, and responsible digital environment.

10.4 Challenges and Opportunities Ahead

The metaverse presents both challenges and opportunities as it continues to evolve. Here are some key challenges and opportunities that lie ahead:

Challenges:

Technical Complexity: Building and maintaining the metaverse involves complex technical requirements, including scalability, interoperability, and ensuring a seamless user experience across various devices and platforms. Overcoming technical challenges while maintaining performance and security will be crucial.

Privacy and Security Concerns: The metaverse raises significant privacy and security concerns. As users engage in virtual environments and interact with others, their personal data and information may be at risk. Protecting user privacy, preventing data breaches, and implementing robust security measures will be essential.

Content Moderation and Governance: The metaverse will require effective content moderation mechanisms to ensure the safety and well-being of users. Establishing governance models that address issues such as harmful content, hate speech, and intellectual property rights will be crucial for maintaining a healthy and inclusive metaverse.

Digital Inclusion and Accessibility: Ensuring that the metaverse is accessible to all individuals, regardless of their socio-economic status, geographic location, or physical abilities, is a critical challenge. Addressing issues of affordability, internet access, and designing inclusive user interfaces will be essential to avoid creating digital divides.

Opportunities:

Economic Growth and Innovation: The metaverse presents immense economic opportunities, with the potential to drive innovation, entrepreneurship, and new business models. The digital economy within the metaverse can generate revenue streams through virtual assets, virtual services, advertising, and virtual marketplaces, creating new jobs and economic growth.

Enhanced Collaboration and Communication: The metaverse can revolutionize collaboration and communication, enabling teams to work together across geographical boundaries. Virtual workspaces, real-time collaboration tools, and immersive communication technologies can improve productivity, efficiency, and creativity in various industries.

Personalized Experiences and Entertainment: The metaverse offers personalized experiences and entertainment options tailored to individual preferences. Users can engage in interactive storytelling, immersive gaming experiences, and virtual events, creating personalized and memorable experiences that go beyond traditional forms of entertainment.

Education and Learning Transformation: The metaverse has the potential to transform education and learning by providing immersive and interactive experiences. Virtual classrooms, educational simulations, and personalized learning environments can enhance student engagement, foster creativity, and provide access to quality education globally.

Social Connections and Community Building: The metaverse can facilitate social connections and community building, bringing together people with shared interests, passions, and identities. Virtual social networks, online communities, and collaborative platforms can foster meaningful interactions and bridge the gap between individuals across the world.

Cultural Exchange and Preservation: The metaverse can facilitate cultural exchange and preservation by recreating historical sites, facilitating virtual travel, and providing platforms for cultural expression. It can enable the sharing of diverse cultural perspectives, traditions, and artistic creations, fostering understanding and appreciation of global cultural heritage.

Addressing the challenges and leveraging the opportunities in the metaverse requires collaboration among various stakeholders, including technology companies, policymakers, researchers, and user communities. By working together, it is possible to create a metaverse that is inclusive, secure, and beneficial to individuals and societies.

Chapter 11. Conclusion

In conclusion, the concept of the metaverse represents a paradigm shift in the way we interact with technology, each other, and the world around us. This book has explored the vast landscape of the metaverse, delving into its origins, technological foundations, social and cultural implications, and the opportunities and challenges it presents.

We have seen how the metaverse has the potential to reshape industries, revolutionize entertainment, education, healthcare, and commerce, and redefine the way we work, collaborate, and socialize. It offers a limitless canvas for creativity, personal expression, and exploration, transcending the limitations of physical space and time.

However, we have also examined the hurdles that need to be overcome in order to fully realize the potential of the metaverse. Privacy and security concerns, content moderation, accessibility, and governance are some of the critical areas that demand attention and thoughtful solutions.

As we look towards the future, it is clear that the metaverse is not just a distant vision, but a reality that is rapidly taking shape. Its evolution will be influenced by technological advancements, societal needs, regulatory frameworks, and the collective choices we make as users, creators, and stakeholders.

The metaverse holds great promise, but its success lies in our ability to shape it responsibly and inclusively. It is up to us to ensure that it remains a space where diverse voices are heard, where privacy and security are protected, and where innovation thrives. Collaboration and open dialogue will be key as we navigate the challenges, seize the opportunities, and build a metaverse that enhances our lives and enriches our human experience.

As you turn the final page of this book, I hope you are inspired to join the journey towards the metaverse, to explore its possibilities, and to contribute to its positive evolution. The future is within our grasp, and the metaverse beckons us to embark on a new era of connectivity, creativity, and collaboration.

11.1 Summary of Key Points

Here is a summary of the key points discussed in this book on the metaverse:

Definition and Overview: The metaverse is a virtual universe that encompasses virtual reality, augmented reality, and the internet, creating immersive and interactive experiences.

Historical Development: The concept of the metaverse has its roots in science fiction but is now becoming a reality due to advancements in technology.

Core Concepts and Characteristics: The metaverse is characterized by virtual environments, social interaction, persistent presence, and user-generated content.

Technological Foundations: The metaverse is built on technologies such as virtual reality, augmented reality, artificial intelligence, blockchain, and cloud computing.

Key Players and Platforms: Major technology companies, startups, and open-source communities are driving the development of the metaverse, with platforms like Facebook Horizon, Roblox, and Decentraland gaining prominence.

Applications: The metaverse has diverse applications in entertainment, gaming, education, healthcare, retail, finance, and more, transforming how we live, work, and interact.

Societal and Cultural Implications: The metaverse presents opportunities for global connectivity, creativity, and cultural exchange, but also raises concerns regarding privacy, security, and digital addiction.

Building the Metaverse: Creating the metaverse requires addressing technical challenges, content creation and curation, user experience design, interoperability, scalability, and security.

Economic Considerations: The metaverse offers new economic models, including virtual economies, digital assets, and monetization strategies through virtual marketplaces and advertising.

Future Trends and Speculations: The metaverse is continuously evolving, with emerging technologies like virtual reality, artificial intelligence, and blockchain expected to shape its future.

Social and Cultural Evolution: The metaverse has the potential to redefine social norms, enable cross-cultural interactions, democratize creativity, and preserve cultural heritage.

Challenges and Opportunities: Challenges include technical complexity, privacy and security concerns, content moderation, and digital inclusion. Opportunities lie in economic growth, enhanced collaboration, personalized experiences, and transformative education.

In conclusion, the metaverse represents a transformative concept that will impact various aspects of our lives. It offers exciting opportunities for innovation and connectivity, but also presents challenges that need to be addressed to ensure a responsible and inclusive metaverse for all.

11.2 Final Thoughts on the Metaverse

The metaverse holds immense promise as a transformative concept that can reshape how we interact with technology, each other, and the world around us. It offers a world of endless possibilities, where virtual and physical realities merge to create immersive and interactive experiences.

However, as we embark on this journey into the metaverse, it is crucial to approach its development with careful consideration and responsible stewardship. We must prioritize privacy and security, ensuring that user data is protected and that individuals have control over their digital identities. Content moderation and governance mechanisms should be established to maintain a safe and inclusive metaverse environment.

The metaverse also presents an opportunity to address societal challenges and bridge divides. It can be a platform for cultural exchange, fostering understanding and appreciation of diverse perspectives. It can democratize access to education, healthcare, and economic opportunities, empowering individuals from all walks of life.

As the metaverse evolves, it will require collaboration among stakeholders, including technology companies, policymakers, researchers, and users. Open dialogue, ethical considerations, and inclusive practices will be essential to shape the metaverse in a way that benefits humanity as a whole.

The metaverse is not just a technological concept; it is a vision of a future where virtual and physical worlds seamlessly coexist, enriching our lives in ways we cannot yet fully comprehend. It invites us to reimagine the boundaries of human experience, creativity, and collaboration.

As we embark on this exciting journey, let us embrace the potential of the metaverse while staying mindful of its impact on individuals, communities, and the broader society. Let us strive to build a metaverse that reflects our shared values, celebrates our diversity, and enhances the human experience in a responsible and inclusive manner.

The future of the metaverse lies in our collective hands, and together, we can shape a world where imagination knows no bounds, connections transcend distance, and opportunities abound for all.

11.3 Call to Action for Individuals and Society

As we enter the era of the metaverse, it is crucial for individuals and society as a whole to actively engage and shape its development. Here is a call to action for individuals and society with respect to the metaverse:

Embrace Learning and Exploration: Take the initiative to learn about the metaverse, its technologies, and its potential applications. Stay informed about the latest developments and trends. Engage in exploration and experimentation to understand its capabilities and implications.

Foster Ethical and Responsible Use: Recognize the ethical considerations and potential societal impacts of the metaverse. Advocate for responsible use, respectful behavior, and adherence to principles of privacy, security, and inclusivity. Contribute to the development of ethical guidelines and best practices.

Demand Privacy and Security: As a user, demand robust privacy and security measures in the metaverse. Understand the data collection and usage policies of platforms and applications you engage with. Support initiatives and technologies that prioritize user data protection and give individuals control over their personal information.

Advocate for Inclusivity and Accessibility: Promote inclusivity in the metaverse by advocating for accessibility features, ensuring that individuals with disabilities can fully participate. Encourage platforms and developers to design user interfaces and experiences that are accessible to diverse populations. Address digital divides and support initiatives that make the metaverse accessible to all.

Engage in Content Creation and Curation: Contribute to the metaverse by actively participating in content creation and curation. Share your ideas, creativity, and talents to enrich the virtual world. Foster a healthy and diverse content ecosystem, ensuring that harmful or inappropriate content is not tolerated.

Support Open Standards and Interoperability: Encourage the adoption of open standards and interoperability among metaverse platforms. Advocate for seamless integration and communication between different virtual environments to enable cross-platform interactions and enhance user experiences.

Collaborate and Engage with Stakeholders: Engage in open dialogue and collaboration with technology companies, policymakers, researchers, and other stakeholders involved in the development of the metaverse. Provide feedback, voice concerns, and contribute to the decision-making processes that shape the metaverse's future.

Prepare for the Future Workforce: Recognize the evolving job landscape in the metaverse and acquire the necessary skills and knowledge to thrive in this new digital frontier. Support educational initiatives that prepare individuals for metaverse-related careers and promote digital literacy.

Foster Digital Well-being: Be mindful of the potential impacts of excessive use and addiction to the metaverse. Prioritize your well-being and maintain a healthy balance between virtual and physical experiences. Promote digital mindfulness and encourage others to do the same.

Advocate for Legal and Regulatory Frameworks: Engage in discussions around the legal and regulatory landscape of the metaverse. Advocate for frameworks that protect user rights, intellectual property, and consumer interests. Support policies that ensure fair competition, prevent monopolistic practices, and safeguard against harmful content.

By actively participating, advocating, and contributing to the development of the metaverse, we can shape it into a vibrant, inclusive, and responsible digital realm that enriches our lives and benefits society as a whole. Together, let us seize the opportunities, address the challenges, and build a metaverse that reflects our shared values and aspirations.

Thank You..........